A FUNEF SERVI

CW01043980

CROSSING THE BAR

A Funeral Service is here to help guide you through what may be the most traumatic and grief-stricken time of your life: Just when the tragedy strikes, you have to think about the details of the Funeral Ceremony and what precedes and follows it.

You will most probably have engaged the services of a well-reputed funeral director, and this book is not to in any way to replace their services.

It is for you to spend a quiet time with family and friends, and give some thought to what may seem small but always important aspects of the Ceremony, before your meeting with your Minister or Celebrant.

- Will you have music, and if so, how will it reflect and celebrate your loved one?
- Perhaps you may wish to have a hymn or a prayer that is special to you or your loved one?
- Should the service be a religious or non-religious one?
- Will there be readings? There are suggested readings in the book to guide you.
- Will you ask for flowers or donations for a charity?

If *A Funeral Service* can take a fraction of the burden from your shoulders, it will have done exactly what is intended.

Paul Hickman

The author sees at first hand just how much comfort families take from readings, poems and prayers at their loved ones' services, some of which are compiled in this book.

To all the authors on behalf of the families, thank you.

Printed in the United Kingdom
First Printing, 2019

ISBN: 978-1-9162411-0-7 (Paperback)
ISBN: 978-1-9162411-1-4 (eBook)

La Palabra Publishing Company Limited
Venture House, The Tanneries
East Street
Titchfield, Hampshire
PO14 4AR

lapalabra.co.uk

ACKNOWLEDGEMENTS

This book would not have happened without the support and encouragement of Molly, Colin, Steve and Rebecca, Jane, Peter and Mary, Greg, Doctor Keith Cleland, and the sheer professionalism of Karen and her team at Librotas.

Special thanks to Craig and Amy for allowing me to use the photo of their beloved George on page 115, along with his sister Bella on page 114.

To all the Funeral Directors, Funeral Arrangers, Conductors and Chapel Attendants, Ministers and Celebrants, throughout the country, we thank each and every one of you for your service.

If a book or guide can be dedicated, then it is to them, and the bereaved we all serve.

66 *Time cannot steal the treasures that we carry in our hearts nor ever dim the shining thoughts our cherished past imparts. And memories of the ones we've loved still cast their gentle glow to grace our day and light our paths wherever we may go.* **99**
– Author unknown

CROSSING THE BAR

Alfred, Lord Tennyson

Sunset and evening star,
And one clear call for me!
And may there be no moaning of the bar,
When I put out to sea,
But such a tide as moving seems asleep,
Too full for sound and foam,
When that which drew from out the
boundless deep turns again home.
Twilight and evening bell, And after that the dark!
And may there be no sadness or farewell, when I embark;
For tho' from out our bourne of Time and
Place the flood may bear me far,
I hope to see my Pilot face to face when I have crost the bar.

CONTENTS

LOSS OF A LOVED ONE

Author unknown

It's a loss, a total, absolute type of missingness that catapults
you into somewhere else, some lost place, where you wander,
where it doesn't seem as though there's light there.
But you will find your way back, you'll go on further, and
you will remember the other places they took you to.
Many other places, of happiness of laughter, you'll
remember those, and then everything between, and
in remembering you'll find them somehow.

THE SERVICE

GRIEF

> **"** *O death, where is your victory?*
> *O death, where is your sting?* **"**
> *– 1 Corinthians 15:55*

When a loved one dies, the sting is of course with those left behind. When grief hits, it's personal, it can shred all our emotions, turn the world upside down, and everyone is unique in the way we can cope with it, and on many occasions struggle to do so.

Nobody can say, "I know how you feel"; they don't. They can empathise with your loss and feelings, but they are not you; they did not have the "actual" personal meaningful relationship you have had over the years with the person you have lost.

Having now sat in over 850 lounges, dining rooms and kitchens with bereaved families, listening to their heart breaking and also uplifting stories, each one is uniquely different to the individuals and members of each family.

I have listened to every form of grief over the years. Nothing can prepare you for the visit when you walk into the house of a family that has lost a loved one. It is quite literally a fresh page, fresh pain, a different life story, unique, every time.

"We want to celebrate our loved one's life", naturally, but still, underlying the celebration is grief in all its forms.

With all this experience, how do I try and describe grief when asked? I heard this apocryphal story many years ago, which, when I thought it through, seemed in my own times of grief and spending time with families, to be near the truth.

Fast flowing river after a major storm

When the storm (*loss of a loved one*) hits suddenly, or perhaps with a storm warning (*protracted illness*), you can fall into this fast flowing river of grief. It can overtake you, swamp you, you don't have the strength to fight the current, and it's overwhelming. You look to the banks of the river to get out, but they are far too steep, and the current keeps taking you faster and further away. You shout for help, assistance please, but others close to you are perhaps caught up in the same torrent. A shoulder to lean on, a hand to hold, ears to listen, you can't get there and the flow is taking you further away.

"How did I get here, life was so straightforward?" The answers just don't come; the current is far too strong.

Then your head goes under the water again when you are not expecting it, causing panic, questions again, how can I survive, my world is suddenly upside down, you're drowning, surely it would be easier just to give up?

But no, "I must keep striving to get to that bank, as there are others that need me", I need to go with the flow to survive, minute by minute, hour by hour, day by day to get through this.

Doubts are formulating, people are trying to help you, well-meaning folk who care about you, but they are helpless, the current is still flowing, encompassing every thought and deed (*when you turn off the light at night, sleep just doesn't come*). The comfort of normality, of routine, looking forward, planning has gone. The only aim is to survive.

However suddenly one day, nobody knows when, the torrent seems to dissipate. There is suddenly hope: you can see the water is becoming shallow and warmer, you can now keep your head above water, you sense normality is close, you can feel it, and then one day you look back.

That torrent that was controlling you has become a trickle; it's now gone, replaced by a gentle breeze on your back and sun on your face, and there is now an opportunity to reach out to others, to start living again. Those shoulders, hands and ears become real.

The memories of the river that build that special bridge of love when loved ones depart and its impact on you will never go away, but life can mean life again, if you are able to embrace it.

There are no time scales for when the river stops flowing, as the river is unique to each one of us.

This easy guide should hopefully assist your family, and ease you through what is such a unique to you painful process, and help to ensure you are comfortable with making your own choices within the comfort of your own surroundings with the selected Funeral Director, and appointed Minister or Celebrant who are there to serve you and your family.

EPITAPH TO A FRIEND – ROBERT BURNS

An honest man here lies at rest,
As e'er God with his image blest;
The friend of man, the friend of truth,
The friend of age, and guide of youth:
Few hearts like his, with virtue warm'd,
Few heads with knowledge so informed;
If there is another world, he lives in bliss;
If there is none, he made the best of this.

STEPS TO GUIDE YOU THROUGH THE PROCESS OF PLANNING A FUNERAL SERVICE

Once a loved one has died, one of the first steps is to visit the local registrar for the death certificate to be issued. When the death certificate is issued, attached to it is a green form which is to be given to the Funeral Director, so the funeral can legally go ahead, and they will then be able to confirm a date for the service.

This could be with a Director your family or friends have used before, one that has been recommended, or possibly the Director has already been appointed due to an insurance funeral plan.

At your visit to the Funeral Director to make the necessary arrangements for either the church, crematorium, or natural burial site, the Director will go through all the logistics and dates best suited for the family, and reserve them.

They will appoint a suitable Celebrant or Minister to conduct the service. If it is a church service it will be a member of the church ministry team selected by the church to conduct the service; this could be a layperson. A Humanist or Celebrant will be appointed for a non-religious service in a crematorium or natural burial site, and possibly a Church Minister or Non-Conformist Minister for services that will include religious content in a crematorium or natural burial site.

Funeral ceremonies may be conducted at churches, crematoriums, public cemeteries, woodland burial grounds, and other burial grounds (subject to restriction).

The Celebrant or Minister appointed by the Funeral Director is, in their experience, the best person to serve your family. You can of course appoint your own, and if you prefer a female Celebrant to a man, or vice versa, then that is your choice.

The appointed Minister or Celebrant will contact the family, and arrange a mutually convenient time for a home visit.

At the visit they will plan the ceremony with you, and if they didn't know the deceased personally, be able to form a rounded picture of your departed family member. This can include their family and friends, their history, work, past times and hobbies. At this stage it may also be important for families to freely discuss various options in relation to procedure during the ceremony.

Detailed preparation prevents reliance on a standard text or format, and in the days leading up to the ceremony, time and care is devoted to writing and compiling a tribute both factually accurate, and with the appropriate tone, by the Minister or Celebrant. If you would like to include humour with funny anecdotal stories, then that can be communicated to the Celebrant.

All Ministers and Celebrants are of course non-judgemental, sympathetic and have wide experience to support you in this time.

By this process, each ceremony can be developed uniquely with families who welcome the opportunity for choice and personal input. A copy of the ceremony or Order of Service can, if requested, be printed for the family, with photographs and readings included. This can also be sent to absent relatives or friends and kept as a memento.

66 When someone you love becomes a memory, the memory becomes a treasure. 99

Memorial ceremonies and also burial of ashes are more usually conducted when some time has elapsed following a funeral. The Funeral Director will organise this on behalf of the family.

PRINTED ORDERS OF SERVICE

The printed Order of Service can form a very important aspect of the service for the family. It is usually in A5 size, of four or eight pages depending on the content of the service.

Orders of Service can be compiled, drafted and printed to order by the Funeral Director or the family if they have the facility to produce their own; in this case it would be given to the Funeral Director, Minister or Celebrant on the day of the service.

Most Ministers and Celebrants will produce a draft copy following their meeting with the family, copied to the Funeral Director if they are producing the Order. The copy also assists the Funeral Director in confirming music choices, and if need be they can finalise the music with crematoriums and their in-house Wesley and Obitus systems, music libraries.

The family can select photographs to be used, and the document will reflect the running order as finalised with the Minister or Celebrant. It should include the words to any hymns selected for the congregation to sing.

Also the words to any poems or readings should be printed, as sometimes, due to the enormity of the occasion, people are not able to take in the significance of the words, and can look at them later and reflect on their meaning.

An invitation and directions to the venue after the service for everybody to get together can be printed on the back cover, together with any requests for donations to a specific charity or charities that are meaningful to the family. These are collected by the Funeral Director and after a set period of time sent directly to the designated charity, which the charity will acknowledge and receipt (these should usually be in cheque format, or online payments if available, as some Funeral Directors may be reluctant to accept cash).

Further information about charitable donations can be found at the end of the book.

THE SERVICE

Timings may vary from one type of service to another. Usually the timings for a crematorium service allow for three pieces of music, plus a hymn or hymns if required for a religious service.

Thirty or forty-five minute services are the norm, but this does include getting the congregation in and seated and leaving the chapel. Double slots are available in most crematoriums, if a large congregation is expected, or a longer service is required by the family. Service times in churches and natural burial sites are not so critical.

A typical service would consist of the following:

- Entrance music as selected by the family.

- A welcome and an explanation of the ceremony will be given by the Celebrant or Minister to the congregation.

- A selected poem or reading.

- Possibly a hymn for a religious service.

- A Tribute or Eulogy to the loved one, mainly biographical. Compiled by the family, it can be delivered often with contributions from family, friends and colleagues. If the family do not feel they can deliver this personally, then the Celebrant will deliver it for them from a prepared script, or the Celebrant will have written their own after the meeting with the family.

- Reflection music can follow the Tribute (if required). This can occur in both religious and non-religious ceremonies.

- A time of reflection for silent meditation or private prayer can follow with the reflection music.

- The Committal or Words of Farewell can then be spoken by the Celebrant, or Commendation and Farewell by a Minister.

- Another appropriate reading or prayer can close the service.

- The service can be concluded with a family invitation to a reception after the service.

- In a crematorium, the exit music can be played and the curtains left open, so the coffin can be seen, and flowers may be placed on it before attendees leave the chapel, or the curtains can close around the coffin as the music plays – whichever the family prefers.

- The family and friends are then traditionally escorted by the Director to the floral tributes.

- After the service, if limousines have been booked by the family, the cars will take the family to the wake.

If there is to be a burial in a public cemetery, there will still be an opportunity to hold a service in the cemetery chapel, including all the above content.

Sometimes a family member may wish to sing a specific song relevant to the family, at any type of service, and this can be planned in accordingly.

Doves can be released after the service, with a poem read out as the doves fly off on release; again the Funeral Director can arrange this.

66 *The song is ended, but the melody lingers on.* 99
— Irving Berlin

A TYPICAL NON-RELIGIOUS ORDER OF SERVICE IN A CREMATORIUM OR NATURAL BURIAL SITE CAN INCLUDE THE FOLLOWING:

Entrance music

Welcome and introduction

Reading or poem

Piece of music

Tribute or Eulogy delivered by a family member or the Celebrant

Reflection music

Reading

Committal and Farewell

Reading or poem

Exit music

A RELIGIOUS ORDER OF SERVICE IN A CHURCH, CREMATORIUM OR NATURAL BURIAL SITE CAN INCLUDE THE FOLLOWING:

Entrance music

Welcome and introduction
Opening prayer
Reading or poem

Hymn (possibly two during the service)

Tribute or Eulogy delivered by a family member or the Minister
Reflection music

Thanksgiving prayer
The Lord's Prayer
Commendation and Farewell
Blessing

Reading
Closing prayer and words
Exit music

Services may take place within a church conducted by a Minister, then a short but dignified Committal can follow at a crematorium. The Funeral Director will book both.

Photographic display

Most crematoriums now have the facility to show family photographs on a screen during the service; selected photos are usually given to the Funeral Director by the family on a USB stick, and they will pass it on to the crematorium prior to the service.

These photos can be shown during the reflection time or during the full service on a loop. It's the family's choice.

Services online

If family members or friends cannot attend the service due to living abroad, working or being unwell and not able to be there in person, some crematoriums have the facility to live stream the service, subject to privacy concerns and access.

For a fee services can be recorded as well, should the family wish to have a long-term memory of the service.

MUSIC SUGGESTIONS FOR SERVICES

MUSIC SUGGESTIONS
FOR SERVICES

Selecting the music and hymns for services in a church, crematorium or natural burial site (most have a chapel) is extremely important to the content of a service for the family.

The traditional format is usually three pieces of selected music that have significant meaning, in honour and memory of the departed loved one: the first piece at the entrance, the second piece after a Tribute or Eulogy for a time of reflection, and the third piece on exit. Although this is just a suggestion, the family of course can select as many pieces as they wish, as long it fits within the specified time frame of the venue, usually 25 or 30 minutes in a crematorium due to other services following on, perhaps longer in a church or natural burial site as there are not the same time constraints.

The following three sections contain over 300 pieces covering a wide range of musical tastes, from pop, to classical, military, hymns and themed music. These pieces are from over 800 services taken in recent years, and each piece of music within the three sections can be used for any one of them. It is the family's own choice; there is no must, as these are guidelines and options to help you make the appropriate personal decisions.

No guide like this could possibly cover every piece of music – that is impossible – and some obvious ones may be missing, which may be because they haven't been used in the 800-plus services I have led.

ENTRY MUSIC

Played during the procession into the chapel or church, with either the congregation seated or standing before the bearers bring the coffin in, or following the coffin as decided by the family. Family members can act as bearers if agreed in advance with the Director.

Popular choices

1. *Albatross* by Fleetwood Mac
2. *Always* by Frank Sinatra
3. *Always and Forever* by Heatwave
4. *And You and I* by Yes
5. *Angels* by Robbie Williams
6. *Autumn Leaves* by Doris Day
7. *Band of Brothers* theme tune
8. *Blanket On the Ground* by Billie Jo Spears
9. *Bye Bye Blackbird* by Sammy Davis Junior
10. *Caribbean Blue* by Enya
11. *Caravan* by Barbara Dixon
12. *Cavatina* by John Williams
13. *Crazy* by Patsy Cline
14. *Death of a Clown* by the Kinks

15. *Dream a Little Dream* by Ella Fitzgerald
16. *Everything I Do* by Bryan Adams
17. *Everything I Own* by Bread
18. *Fields of Gold* by Eva Cassidy
19. *Flower of Scotland* by the Black Watch Pipe Band
20. *Guardian Angels* by Mario Lanza
21. *Hallelujah* by Katherine Jenkins or Jeff Buckley
22. *Here's to Life* by Barbra Streisand
23. *Hero* by Mariah Carey
24. *Holding Back the Years* by Simply Red
25. *I Just Called to Say I Love You* by Stevie Wonder
26. *I'll Never Find Another You* by Billy Fury
27. *I'll Walk with God* by Mario Lanza
28. *I'm Your Angel* by Celine Dion and R. Kelly
29. *Like I've Never Been Gone* by Billy Fury
30. *Little Old Wine Drinker Me* by Dean Martin
31. *Living on a Prayer* by Bon Jovi
32. *Mama* by the Spice Girls
33. *Memory Number One* by Webb Pierce
34. *Moonlight Serenade* by Glenn Miller
35. *Moon River* by Audrey Hepburn
36. *Morning Has Broken* by Cat Stevens
37. *Never Find Another You* by Billy Fury
38. *Never Tear Us Apart* by Paloma Faith
39. *Nightingale Serenade* by Andre Rieu

65. *Unchained Melody* by the Righteous Brothers
66. *What a Wonderful World* by Louis Armstrong
67. *What Becomes of the Broken Hearted* by Jimmy Ruffin
68. *When I Fall in Love* by Nat King Cole
69. *Where My Heart Will Take Me* by Enterprise
70. *Where We Never Grow Old* by Jim Reeves
71. *White Dreams* by Fairport Convention
72. *With or Without You* by U2
73. *You Are My Sunshine* by Anne Murray
74. *You Are Not Alone* by Michael Jackson
75. *You Raise Me Up* by Westlife
76. *You'll Be in My Heart* by Phil Collins

Classical choices

1. Albinoni's *Adagio in G Minor*
2. *Amazing Grace* by the Scots Guards
3. *Ave Maria* by Maria Callas
4. *Canzonetta Sull'aria* from Mozart's The Marriage of Figaro (the music from the film Shawshank Redemption)
5. *Guardian Angels* by Mario Lanza

6. *Humoresques* by Dvorak
7. *I Vow to Thee My Country* by Katherine Jenkins
8. *LIlll Bolero* by The Band of the Royal Electrical and Mechanical Engineers
9. *Moonlight Sonata* by Beethoven
10. *Morning Mood* from Ibsen's Peer Gynt Suite No. 1, Op. 46
11. *Nimrod* by Elgar
12. *Nearer My God to Thee* by Andre Rieu
13. *Pearl Fishers Duet – Euphoniums* by David and Robert Childs
14. *Sheep May Safely Graze* by J.S. Bach
15. *Spring* by Vivaldi
16. *The Lark Ascending* by Vaughan Williams
17. *The Old Rugged Cross* by Alan Jackson
18. *The Shepherd's Song*, 5th Movement of Beethoven's 6th Symphony
19. *Vide Cor Meum (See My Heart)* sung by Katherine Jenkins

66 *Time is too slow for those who wait; Too swift for those who fear; Too long for those who grieve; Too short for those who rejoice; But for those that love; Time is eternity.* 99
– Henry Van Dyke

REFLECTION MUSIC

These pieces usually follow a Tribute or Eulogy, either delivered by the Celebrant or a member of the family, to allow them to reflect on the words spoken. If time allows more than one piece of reflection music can be planned in.

Popular choices

1. *Always On My Mind* by Elvis Presley
2. *Amazed* by Lonestar
3. *Amazing Grace* by Hayley Westenra
4. *Amazing Grace* by Johnny Cash
5. *Angel in Blue* by General Lafayette
6. *Annie's Song* by John Denver
7. *As Time Goes By* by the Mantovani Orchestra
8. *Beautiful Soul* by Cindy Campo
9. *Because You Loved Me* by Celine Dion
10. *Beyond the Sea* by Frank Sinatra
11. *Blowing in the Wind* by Bob Dylan
12. *Candle in the Wind* by Elton John
13. *Candle Song* by Jon Anderson
14. *Can You Feel the Love Tonight* by John Barrowman

15. *Chasing Cars* by Snow Patrol
16. *Cherish* by Cool and the Gang
17. *Close Your Eyes* by Michael Bublé
18. *Dance with My Father* by Luther Vandross
19. *Dance of the Lambs* by Kim Robertson
20. *Danny Boy* by Celtic Woman
21. *Dreams* by Gabrielle
22. *Endless Love* by the New Reflection Orchestra
23. *Ever Green* by Will Young
24. *Everywhere* by Fleetwood Mac
25. *Father and Son* by Boyzone
26. *Funny Face* by Donna Fargo
27. *God Only Knows How I Feel About You* by the Beach Boys
28. *Going Back* by Dusty Springfield
29. *Goodbye is the Saddest Word* by Celine Dion
30. *Have I Told You Lately That I Love You* by Van Morrison
31. *Heart of Gold* by Neil Young
32. *Heaven Was Needing a Hero* by Jo Dee Messina
33. *Here With Me* by Dido
34. *Holding Back the Years* by Simply Red
35. *Holy Overshadowing* by Graham Kendrick
36. *How Do I Love You* by LeAnn Rimes
37. *How Great Thou Art* by Elvis Presley
38. *I Believe* by the Bachelors
39. *I Can't Stop Loving You* by Elvis Presley
40. *I Dreamed I Was in Heaven* by Charlie Landsborough

41. *If I Should Die Tonight* by Marvin Gaye
42. *If Tomorrow Never Comes* by Garth Brooks
43. *I Just Want to Dance With You* by Daniel O'Donnell
44. *I Know You Care* by Ellie Goulding
45. *I Need You* by Danielle O'Donnell
46. *I Still Miss You* by Keith Anderson
47. *I Think I'm Going Back* by Dusty Springfield
48. *I Will Always Love You* by Whitney Houston
49. *I'll Be Seeing You* by Rosemary Clooney
50. *I'll Never Find Another You* by Billy Fury
51. *I'll See You Again* by Westlife
52. *In Dreams* by Roy Orbison
53. *In My Life* by the Beatles
54. *In My Mother's Arms* by Dame Vera Lynn
55. *In the Arms of an Angel* by Susan Boyle
56. *Into the West* by Annie Lennox
57. *Jealous of the Angels* by Jenn Bostic
58. *Keep Me in Your Heart for a While* by Warren Zevon
59. *Knock, Knock, Knocking on Heaven's Door* by Bob Dylan
60. *Life Is a Rollercoaster* by Ronan Keating
61. *Little Darling* by Marvin Gaye
62. *Living the Years* by Mike and the Mechanics
63. *Local Hero* by Dire Straits
64. *Love Changes Everything* by Michael Ball

THE SERVICE

MUSIC

POEMS, PRAYERS & READINGS

89. *Somewhere Only We Know* by Lily Allen
90. *Somewhere Over the Rainbow* by Israel Kamakawiwo'ole
91. *Stars* by Simply Red
92. *Stranger on the Shore* by Acker Bilk
93. *Summertime* by Sidney Bechet
94. *Teardrops* by Womack and Womack
95. *Thank You for Being a Friend* by Andrew Gold
96. *The First Time Ever I Saw Your Face* by Roberta Flack
97. *The Power of Love* by Celine Dion
98. *The Prayer* by Russell Watson and Lulu
99. *The Rose* by Bette Midler or Elaine Page
100. *The Way We Were* by Barbra Streisand
101. *The Wonder of You* by Elvis Presley
102. *That's Amore* by Dean Martin
103. *Thinking Out Loud* by Ed Sheeran
104. *Time After Time* by Cyndi Lauper
105. *True Love* by Bing Crosby and Grace Kelly
106. *Unforgettable* by Nat King Cole
107. *Up Where We Belong* by Joe Cocker
108. *We Have All the Time in the World* by Louis Armstrong
109. *What Colour is the Wind* by Charlie Landsborough
110. *What Makes You Beautiful* by One Direction
111. *When Irish Eyes Are Smiling* by Ruby Murray
112. *Where Do I Begin* by Andy Williams
113. *Who Knew* by Pink
114. *Who Wants to Live Forever* by Queen

115. *With a Little Help from My Friends* by Joe Cocker
116. *Woman in Love* by Barbra Streisand
117. *Wonderful Life* by Black
118. *You Belong to Me* by Patsy Cline
119. *You Bring the Sun Out* by Randy Crawford
120. *You Can Close Your Eyes* by James Taylor
121. *You Fill Up My Senses* by John Denver
122. *You Raise Me Up* by Westlife
123. *You'll Be in My Heart* by Phil Collins
124. *You'll Never Be Forgotten* by Jessica Andrews
125. *You'll Never Walk Alone* by Gerry and the Pacemakers
126. *You're My Best Friend* by Queen

Classical and musicals

1. *Air on a G String* by Johann Sebastian Bach
2. *All in an April Evening* by the Glasgow Orpheus Choir
3. *Amazing Grace* by Celtic Woman
4. *Ashokan Farewell* by Jay Ungar
5. *Be My Love* by Mario Lanza
6. *Bolero* by Ravel
7. *Bring Him Home* by Alfie Boe
8. *By the Sleepy Lagoon* by Eric Coates (instrumental)

9. *Cantique de Jean Racine (Fauré)* by Cambridge Singers
10. *Dreams of Love* by Franz Liszt
11. *Empty Chairs and Empty Tables* from Les Miserables
12. *Flower Duet* by Katherine Jenkins
13. *I Dreamed a Dream* from Les Miserables
14. *I'll Walk with God* by Mario Lanza
15. *Jesu Joy of Man's Desiring* by J.S. Bach
16. *Lullaby in Ragtime* by Nilsson
17. *Lullaby of Broadway* by Jerry Orbach
18. *Old Man River* by Paul Robeson
19. *Pachelbel's Canon* in D Major
20. *Panis Angelicus* by Kiri Te Kanawa
21. *Piano Sonata No. 14 (Moonlight)* by Beethoven
22. *Pie Jesu* by Sarah Brightman or Katherine Jenkins
23. *Requiem* by Charlotte Church
24. *Requiem – Lacrimosa* by Mozart
25. *Suo Gan* by Charlotte Church (Empire of the Sun)
26. *The Prayer* by Andrea Bocelli and Katherine McPhee
27. *The Walk to the Paradise Garden* by Brigg Fair
28. *Voice of an Angel* by Charlotte Church
29. *You Raise Me Up* by Andre Rieu

EXIT MUSIC

Played at the end of the service when the family say their last goodbyes and leave the chapel or church. In a crematorium the family can decide if they wish to have the curtains closed or remaining open when the exit music is playing.

Popular choices

1. *A Rockin' Good Way* by Brook Benton and Dinah Washington
2. *All I Can Say is Goodbye* by Tom Jones
3. *Another One Bites* the Dust by Queen
4. *Beggar on a Beach of Gold* by Mike and the Mechanics
5. *Bless You Sister* by Bix Beiderbecke
6. *Blue Velvet* by Bobby Vinton
7. *Born to Love You* by Queen
8. *Carnival de Venice* by Andre Rieu
9. *Take Me Home, Country Roads* by John Denver

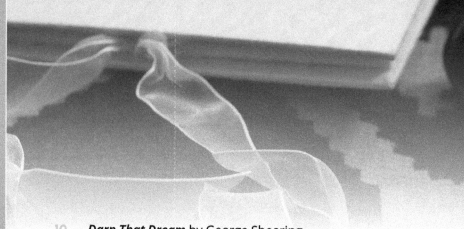

10. ***Darn That Dream*** by George Shearing
11. ***Don't Let the Sun Go Down On Me*** by Elton John and George Michael
12. ***Dream a Little Dream*** by Ella Fitzgerald and Louis Armstrong
13. ***English Country Garden*** by Jimmie Rodgers
14. ***English Rose*** by Paul Weller
15. ***Everybody Hurts*** by REM
16. ***Every Time We Say Goodbye*** by Ella Fitzgerald
17. ***Flying Without Wings*** by Westlife
18. ***Funny Face I Love You*** by Donna Fargo
19. ***Going Home*** by Mark Knopler
20. ***Going Out Dancing*** by Rod Stewart
21. ***Going Underground*** by The Jam
22. ***Goodbye Is the Saddest Word*** by Celine Dion
23. ***Greensleeves*** by the Mantovani Orchestra
24. ***He Ain't Heavy He's My Brother*** by the Hollies
25. ***Home By the Sea*** by Genesis
26. ***Honey*** by Bobby Goldberg
27. ***How Do I Live*** by LeAnn Rimes
28. ***I Believe*** by Gordon McRae
29. ***I Don't Want To Set the World On Fire*** by the Ink Spots
30. ***I Made It Through the Rain*** by Barry Manilow
31. ***I Remember You*** by Frank Ifield
32. ***I Wasn't Expecting That*** by Jamie Lawson

33. *I Would Walk 500 Miles* by The Proclaimers
34. *If I Could Turn Back the Hands of Time* by R. Kelly
35. *In the Arms of an Angel* by Sarah Malaccan
36. *I'll Be Missing You* by Puff Daddy
37. *I'll Be On My Way* by the Straw Doctors
38. *I'll Never Stop Loving You* by Doris Day
39. *Iris* by the Goo Goo Dolls
40. *I've Had the Time of My Life* by Bill Medley
41. *Let It Be* by the Beatles
42. *Let Me Go* by Gary Barlow
43. *Losing My Religion* by REM
44. *Lucky Man* by the Verve
45. *Memories* by Elvis Presley
46. *My Heart Will Go On* by Celine Dion
47. *My Way* by Frank Sinatra
48. *Only You* by the Platters
49. *On the Road Again* by Willie Nelson
50. *Paint the Sky with Stars* by Enya
51. *Pick Up the Pieces* by the Average White Band
52. *Please Release Me* by Engelbert Humperdinck
53. *Please Remember* by LeAnn Rimes
54. *Purple Heather* by Rod Stewart
55. *Que Sera Sera* by Doris Day
56. *Riders on the Storm* by The Doors
57. *Sailor Stop Your Roaming* by Petula Clark

58. *See You When I See You* by Jason Aldean
59. *Sex Bomb* by Tom Jones
60. *She's a Lady* by Tom Jones
61. *Simply the Best* by Tina turner
62. *Smile* by Westlife
63. *So Long Farewell* from The Sound of Music
64. *Softly As I Leave You* by Matt Monro
65. *Spring Time* by Felix Mendelssohn
66. *Stand By Me* by the Drifters
67. *Stop Crying Your Eyes Out* by Oasis
68. *Take Five* by Dave Brubeck
69. *Thank You for the Days* by Kirsty MacColl
70. *Thank You for the Music* by Abba
71. *That's Life* by Frank Sinatra
72. *The Last Waltz* by Engelbert Humperdinck
73. *The One I Love* by David Grey
74. *The Rose* by Conway Twitty
75. *The Show Must Go* On by Queen
76. *There Goes My Everything* by Engelbert Humperdinck
77. *There You Will Be* by Faith Hill
78. *This Is My Life* by Dame Shirley Bassey

79. *Time to Say Goodbye (Con Te Partiro)* by Andrea Bocelli/ Sarah Brightman/Il Divo
80. *Top of the World* by the Carpenters
81. *True Love Ways* by Buddy Holly
82. *Use Somebody* by Kings of Leon
83. *Wand'rin Star* by Lee Marvin
84. *Wanderer* by Dion and the Belmonts
85. *We'll Be Together Again* by Frank Sinatra
86. *When Will I See You Again* by Diana Ross
87. *Who Wants to Live Forever* by Queen
88. *Wind Beneath My Wings* by Paula MacAskill
89. *Wings of a Butterfly* by Jimmy Scott
90. *Wish You Were Here* by Pink Floyd
91. *Without You* by Harry Nilsson
92. *World's Greatest* by R. Kelly
93. *You'll Never Walk Alone* by Gerry and the Pacemakers
94. *Young Hearts Run Free* by Candi Staton
95. *Your Song* by Elton John
96. *You've Got the Love* by Florence and the Machine

66 *Weep if you must, parting is hell, but life goes on. So sing as well.* 99
— Joyce Grenfell

Classical and big band

1. *Cantata* by J.S. Bach
2. *Concerto de Arranjuez* by Rodrigo
3. *I Dreamed a Dream* by Andre Rieu
4. *In the Mood* by the Glenn Miller Band
5. *Jesu Joy of Man's Desiring* by Bach
6. *Moonlight Serenade* by the Glenn Miller Band
7. *Narcissus* by Ethelbert Nevin
8. *New World Symphony, Largo* by Dvorak
9. *One Fine Day* by Giacomo Puccini (from Madame Butterfly)
10. *String of Pearls* by Glenn Miller
11. *Sugar Foot Stomp* by Benny Goodman
12. *We'll Meet Again* by Dame Vera Lynn
13. *When the Saints Go Marching in* by Chris Barber
14. *Wish Me Luck as You Wave Me Goodbye* by Dame Vera Lynn
15. *The Scouting Hymn*

MILITARY BANDS

(can also be used for entrance music)

1. *Abide with Me, Evening Hymn and Last Post*, by the Band of Her Majesty's Royal Marines
2. *A Life on the Ocean Waves* by the Band of Her Majesty's Royal Marines
3. *Boogie Woogie Bugle Boy of Company B* by The Andrews Sisters
4. *Cockleshell Heroes* by the Band of Her Majesty's Royal Marines
5. *Farmer's Boy* by the Band of the Royal Hampshire Regiment
6. *Flower of Scotland* by the Black Watch Pipe Band
7. *Hearts of Oak* by the Band of the Royal Navy
8. *High on a Hill* by the Band of Somerset Light Infantry
9. *Lilli Bolero*, the March of the REME

10. *Royal Air Force March Past* by the Central Band of the RAF
11. *The Dam Busters* by the Band of the Royal Air Force
12. *Sarie Marais*, the Royal Marines Commando March
13. *Scipio* by the Band of the Cold Stream Guards (slow march)

❝ *Those we love don't go away, they walk beside us every day, Unseen, unheard, but always near, Still loved, still missed and very dear.* **❞**
– Author unknown

THEMED OR HUMOROUS MUSIC

1. *Always Look on the Bright Side* by Monty Python
2. *Bob the Builder* theme
3. *Bring Me Sunshine* by Morecambe and Wise
4. *Dad's Army* theme
5. *Gone Fishing* by Bing Crosby
6. *Goodbye* by Peter Cook and Dudley Moore
7. *Kiss Me Goodnight Sergeant Major* by Vera Lynn
8. *Last of the Summer Wine* theme
9. *Little Old Wine Drinker Me* by Dean Martin
10. *Only Fools and Horses* theme
11. *Pub with No Beer* by Slim Dusty
12. *Rock Around the Clock* by Bill Haley and the Comets
13. *Ship Ahoy (All the Nice Girls Love a Sailor)* by Ella Retford
14. *Straight Down the Middle* by Bing Crosby
15. *They Are Coming to Take Me Away* by Napoleon XIV
16. *The Ying Tong Song* by the Goons

HYMNS

1. *Abide with Me* by Henry Francis Lyte
2. *All Things Bright and Beautiful* by Cecil Francis Alexander (1818–1895)
3. *Amazing Grace* by John Newton (1725–1827)
4. *And Did Those Feet in Ancient Times* by William Blake (1757–1827)
5. *Bread of Heaven* by John Hughes (1873–1932)
6. *Dear Lord and Father of Mankind* by John Greenleaf Whittier (1807–1892)
7. *He Who Would Valiant Be* by John Bunyan
8. *How Great Thou Art* by Stuart K. Hine (1899–1989, c 1953)
9. *Immortal Invisible God Only Wise* by W. Chalmers Smith (1824–1908)
10. *Lead Us Heavenly Father Lead Us* by James Edmeston (1791–1867)
11. *Lord of the Dance* by Sidney Carter
12. *Morning Has Broken Like the First Morning* by Eleanor Farjeon (1881–1965)
13. *Praise My Soul the King of Heaven* by Henry Francis Lyte (1793–1847)

14. ***The Day Thou Gavest Lord is Ended*** by John Ellerton (1826–1893)
15. ***The Lord's My Shepherd, I'll Not Want***, Scottish Psalter 1650
16. ***There Is a Green Hill Far Away*** by Cecil Frances Alexander (1818–1895)

Military

1. ***Royal Navy – Eternal Father, Strong to Save*** by William Whiting (1825–1878)

YOU ARE NEAR

66 *You are near, even if we don't see you. You are with us, even if you are far away you are in our hearts, in our thoughts, in our lives, always.* **99**
– Author unknown

MOST POPULAR

Most popular music selections which can be used at any time during the service.

1. *Albatross* by Fleetwood Mac
2. *Always Look on the Bright Side* by Monty Python
3. *Bring Me Sunshine* by Morecambe and Wise
4. *Cavatina* (the theme from The Deer Hunter)
5. *Dance With My Father* by Luther Vandross
6. *Going Out Dancing* by Rod Stewart
7. *I Don't Want to Set the World On Fire* by the Ink Spots
8. *Knock, Knock, Knocking on Heaven's Door* by Bob Dylan
9. *Let Me Go* by Gary Barlow
10. *Moonlight Serenade* by Glenn Miller
11. *My Heart Will Go On* by Celine Dion
12. *My Way* by Frank Sinatra
13. *Nimrod* by Elgar
14. *On the Wings of an Angel* by Sarah McLaughlin
15. *Pachelbel's Canon in D Major*
16. *Simply the Best* by Tina Turner
17. *Smile* by Nat King Cole
18. *Softly As I Leave You* by Matt Monro
19. *Strangers On the Shore* by Acker Bilk
20. *The Last Waltz* by Engelbert Humperdinck
21. *Time to Say Goodbye* by Andrea Bocelli, Sarah Brightman or Il Divo
22. *Unforgettable* by Nat King Cole
23. *We'll Meet Again* by Dame Vera Lynn
24. *Wish Me Luck As You Wave Me Goodbye* by Dame Vera Lynn
25. *With or Without You* by U2
26. *Who Wants to Live Forever* by Queen

MUSIC CHOICES –
NO SET RULES

There is no right or wrong piece of music for each aspect of the service. The ones selected by the family are always the right ones.

The following true story about a family making their music choices hopefully confirms this.

Asked to take the service of a lady who had sadly passed away, and given the contact details of the widower, I met with this lovely gentleman who had been married to his best friend and soulmate for over 60 years, together with his daughter, and granddaughter.

Over coffee around the kitchen table, we planned the burial service, with the celebration and thanksgiving in the chapel.

All was dutifully planned and then we arrived at the exit music prior to processing out.

When asked the music selection for the exit of the chapel, the widower proclaimed, "I want a piece by Tom Jones to exit."

I replied, "'It's Not Unusual', ha ha, or is that 'Green Green Grass of Home'?"

"No it's *'S-x Bomb'*," he loudly proclaimed. At that the daughter exclaimed, "Dad you can't." "But your mother loved 'S—'", he responded with a straight face. At that comment, which drew breaths and laughter in equal measure, the granddaughter, horrified at the thought her grandparents actually indulged in such matters, exclaimed loudly, ***"Granddad!"***

"She did, and that is what we are going to have," was his reply.

The meeting was concluded with hugs and tears all round (some laughter ones) and the Order of Service was produced, with exit music just titled "Tom Jones".

As instructed, I introduced the "melancholy" exit music by Tom Jones, looking at the gentleman, only to see him shaking with laughter, with him knowing what was about to happen. His daughter and granddaughter had eyes raised to the heavens and were shaking their heads.

When the music started, I have never seen so many mouths open wide in astonishment; it was priceless, and tears were rolling down the widower's cheeks, laughter mixed with grief.

The service was conducted, and the mourners left.

About a month later, I met with the widower and received the biggest hug ever, and these words will always remain with me.

"That was an amazing celebration of my beautiful wife's life, thank you so much." *This piece was the right piece.*

POEMS, PRAYERS
& READINGS

NON-RELIGIOUS POEMS AND READINGS

Poems and readings can reflect so many aspects of the family member who has left us: their personalities (perhaps fun loving, military, or family orientated), priorities (hobbies), experiences (travel), achievements (work) and relationships.

Religious and non-religious texts in a reading can be the best way to portray the personality and life experiences of the departed, and the overwhelming feeling of loss, but also the pride of the family and friends.

A family member or friend can feel an integral part of the service by actually reading at it, without the pressure of delivering a personal tribute to the departed. If nobody does come forward the officiant can read it on their behalf. To follow is just a selection, to perhaps help and guide you to decide what is best for your family.

Sadly due to copyright restrictions it has not been possible to include all the words to some of the poems and readings. So where possible I have given a pointer towards other relevant and suitable poems and readings within the sections of the book, which can be further resourced online.

I honour and thank all the authors whose material is included in this book, as they have created material that is of great help and support to so many families at this time of great need.

Due to the aforementioned copyright issues, where "......More" appears, please refer to suggested websites at the end of the poems and readings section. By searching on the name of the reading and the author's name on a poem-based website you will be able to read the full poem to see if it is relevant for your family.

HONOURED FAMILY MEMBER
Lori Boast

A light from our family is gone
A voice we loved is stilled
A place is vacant in the home
which never can be filled

We have to mourn the loss of one
we would've love to keep
but God who surely loved her best
Has finally made her sleep

After a lifetime of her love and joy
And music to fill our ears
God leaves these wondrous memories
to help us through our tears

LORD OF POTS AND PANS

Author unknown. A poem written by a 19-year-old girl in domestic service in England

Lord of all pots and pans and things,
Since I've no time to be
A saint by doing lovely things or
Watching late with thee,
Or dreaming in the twilight or
Storming heaven's gates.
Make me a saint by getting meals or
Washing up the plates.

Although I must have Martha's hands,
I have Mary's mind, and,
When I black the boots and shoes
Thy sandals, Lord, I find.
I think of how they trod the earth
what time I scrub the floor,
accept this meditation, Lord,
I haven't time for more.

Warm all the kitchen with thy love,
and light it with thy peace,
forgive me all my worrying
and make all grumbling cease.
Thou who didst love to give men food
in room or by the sea
Accept this service that I do
I do it unto thee.

> **66** *This is my simple religion. No need for temples. No need for complicated philosophy. Your own mind, your own heart is the temple. Your philosophy is simple kindness.* **99**
> *— Dalai Lama XIV*

A FAMILY IS LIKE A CIRCLE

Nicole M. O'Neal

A family is like a circle, the connection never ends,
And even if at times it breaks, in time it always mends.
A family is like the stars, Somehow they're always there

......More

A FALLEN LIMB

Author unknown

A limb has fallen from the family tree.
I keep hearing a voice that says, "Grieve not for me.
Remember the best times, the laughter, and the song.
The good life I lived while I was strong.
Continue my heritage, I'm counting on you. Keep
smiling and surely the sun will shine through.
My mind is at ease, my soul is at rest.
Remembering all, how I truly was blessed.
Continue traditions, no matter how small.
Go on with your life, don't worry about falls
I miss you all dearly, so keep up your chin.
Until the day comes we're together again."

AFTERGLOW

Helen Lowrie Marshall

I'd like the memory of me to be a happy one.
I'd like to leave an afterglow of smiles when life is done. I'd
like to leave an echo whispering softly down the ways

......More

ANGEL CORD

Author unknown

We are connected, my child and I,
by an invisible cord, not seen by the eye.
It's not like the cord that connects us 'til birth.
This cord can't be seen by anyone on earth.
This cord does its work right from the start.
It binds us together attached to my heart.
I know that it's there, though no one can see,
the invisible cord from my child to me.
The strength of this cord is hard to describe,
it can't be destroyed, it can't be denied.

It's stronger than any cord man could create.
It withstands the test and can hold any weight.
Though you are gone and not here with me,
The cord is still there but no one can see.
It pulls at my heart, I am bruised, I am sore.
But this cord is my lifeline as never before.
I am thankful that God connects us this way.
A mother and child, nothing can take it away.

DEATH IS NOTHING AT ALL
Henry Scott Holland

Death is nothing at all, I have only slipped away into the next room. I am I and you are you. Whatever we were to each other that we are still. Call me by my old familiar name. Speak to me in the easy way you always used. Put no difference into your tone. Wear no forced air of solemnity or sorrow. Laugh as we always laughed at the little jokes we always enjoyed together. Play, smile, think of me, pray for me, and let my name be ever the household word that it always was. Let it be spoken without effort without the ghost of a shadow in it.

Life means all that it ever meant. It is the same as it ever was. There is absolute unbroken continuity. What is death but a negligible accident? Why should I be out of mind because I am out of sight? I am waiting for you, for an interval, somewhere very near, just around the corner. All is well. Nothing is hurt; nothing is lost. One brief moment and all will be as it was before. How we shall laugh at the trouble of parting when we meet again!

FAR AWAY
Author unknown

Far away, I can't see you. You're gone forever, I won't see you again, you're the one I loved, and I wish you were here. You're gone forever. Where did you go, I need you now. You're gone forever.

Are you dead? I hope you aren't. I love you. Are you a ghost? I can't hold your hand. You're gone forever.

It's like you are a ghost, my hand just goes through your hand. It's not fair. Where are you!! You're gone forever.

FEEL NO GUILT IN LAUGHTER

Author unknown

Feel no guilt in laughter; he knows how much you care.
Feel no sorrow in a smile that he is not here to share. You
cannot grieve forever; he would not want you to. He'd
hope that you could carry on the way you always do.

So, talk about the good times and the way you showed you cared,
the days you spent together, all the happiness you shared.

Let memories surround you, a word someone may say
will suddenly recapture a time, an hour, a day, that
brings him back as clearly as though he were still here,
and fills you with the feeling that he is always near.

For if you keep those moments, you will never be apart, and
he will live forever, locked safely within your heart.

FIVE MINUTES

Annmarie Campbell

If I only had five minutes the day you passed away, I would
have had time to tell you all the things I needed to say

......More

FUNERAL BLUES

W.H. Auden

Stop all the clocks, cut off the telephone,
Prevent the dog from barking with a juicy bone.
Silence the pianos and with muffled drum
Bring out the coffin, let the mourners come.

Let aeroplanes circle moaning overhead
Scribbling on the sky the message "*He/she* is Dead",
Put crêpe bows round the white necks of the public doves,
Let the traffic policemen wear black cotton gloves.

He/she was *my/our* North, *my/our* South, *my/our* East and West,
My/our working week and *my/our* Sunday rest,
My/our noon, *my/our* midnight, *my/our* talk, *my/our* song,
I/we thought that love would last forever: *I/we was/were* wrong

The stars are not wanted now, put out every one;
Pack up the moon and dismantle the sun;
Pour away the ocean and sweep up the wood.
For nothing now can ever come to any good.

HIS/HER JOURNEY'S JUST BEGUN

Ellen Brenneman

His journey's just begun, don't think of him as
gone away, his journey's just begun,
life holds so many facets, this earth is only one

......More

GO PLACIDLY (DESIDERATA)

Max Ehrmann

Go placidly amid the noise and haste, and remember what peace
there may be in silence. As far as possible without surrender
be on good terms with all persons.
Speak your truth quietly and clearly;
and listen to others, even the dull and the
ignorant; they too have their story

......More

I HEARD YOUR VOICE IN THE WIND TODAY

Tim Edds

I heard your voice in the wind today and I turned to see your face;
the warmth of the wind caressed me as I stood silently in place.
I felt your touch in the sun today as its warmth filled the sky

......More

I FALL ASLEEP

Samuel Butler

I fall asleep in the full and certain hope
That my slumber shall not be broken;
And that though I be all-forgetting,
Yet shall I not be forgotten,
But continue that life in the thoughts
and deeds of those I loved.

REMEMBER ME

Anthony Dowson

Speak of me as you have always done.
Remember the good times, laughter, and fun.
Share the happy memories we've made.
Do not let them wither or fade.
I'll be with you in the summer's sun

......More

I LIVE ON
Author unknown

Don't cry for me in sadness; don't weep for me in sorrow,
for I will be beside you, as sure as comes tomorrow.
My body has gone but my spirit lives on, as does my love for
you. Just as in life. I'll watch over you, I always will be true.
My blood lives on in my children, how I've
watched them grow up with pride.
I'll live on within them, always by their side.
I know my jokes weren't always funny and jobs weren't always done.
Just try and always remember the good
times, the days when we had fun.
Reach out if you need me, for I will always be near.
Just talk to me, as if I am there, I promise I will hear.
For I'll live on, within your mind, we'll never be apart,
As long as you keep my memory, deep within your heart.
So lift up your hearts, don't be sad, my spirit hasn't gone.
While you're still there, so am I, I really will live on.

IF I SHOULD GO
Joyce Grenfell

If I should go before the rest of you
Break not a flower nor inscribe a stone
Nor when I'm gone speak in a Sunday voice

......More

I THOUGHT OF YOU WITH LOVE TODAY

Author unknown

I thought of you with love today
but that is nothing new
I thought about you yesterday
and days before that too,
I think of you in silence
...I often speak your name
All I have are memories
and your picture in a frame
Your memory is my keepsake
with which I'll never part
God has you in His keeping
I have you in my heart.

JUST A BREATH AWAY

Marilyn Ferguson

Look for me in springtime
As raindrops fill the air
In the splendour of the rainbow
You'll find my presence there.
You will find me in the fragrance
Of April's sweet perfume...
On the distant sound of the thunder
In the gently swaying trees.
In the golden fields of harvest
is where I can be found

......More

ONE LITTLE ROSE
Author unknown

I would rather have one little rose
from the garden of a friend
than to have the choicest flowers
When my stay on earth must end.

I would rather have one pleasant word
in kindness said to me
than flattery when my heart is still
and life has ceased to be.

I would rather have a loving smile
from friends I know are true
than tears shed round my casket
when this world I've bid adieu.

Bring me all your flowers today
whether pink, or white, or red;
I'd rather have one blossom now
than a truckload when I'm dead.

SMILING IS INFECTIOUS
Author unknown

Smiling is infectious, you catch it like the flu, when someone smiled at me today, I started smiling too. I passed around the corner and someone saw my grin. When he smiled I realised I'd passed it on to him. I thought about that smile, then I realised its worth. A single smile, just like mine could travel round the earth. So, if you feel a smile begin, don't leave it undetected. Let's start an epidemic quick, and get the world infected!

BEAUTIFUL MEMORIES
Author unknown

A bouquet of beautiful memories,
Sprayed with a million tears
Wishing God could have spared you,
If just for a few more years.
We love you, we miss you and
we are proud to keep your dream and vision alive.

I AM MOVING ON
Author unknown

I am moving on
Reaching toward my hopes and dreams,
it has taken me far too long to reach this place, it seems.
My fears may try to hold me back to try and block my way
But with courage and faith in my heart,
I will get there come what may.

The road will be a long one, and it may be rocky, too.
But when I reach this place in time
My dreams could all shine through.

I am coming nearer to my goals.
And my excitement grows,
the plans I have made will soon be real
Along with the destiny I chose.

Though I have been tossed and turned in life's storms
I will surely see a brighter dawn
I'm no longer held back by my fears
I'm finally.... Moving on.

I LAY MY HEAD TO REST
Author unknown

I lay my head to rest and in doing so
lay at your feet the faces I have seen
the voices I have heard, the words I have spoken,
the hands I have shaken, the service I have given
the joys I have shared, the sorrows revealed
I lay them at your feet and in doing so lay my head to rest

A LIFE WELL-LIVED
Author unknown

A life well-lived is a precious gift
of hope and strength and grace
from someone who has made our world
a brighter, better place.

It is filled with moments, sweet and sad
with smiles and with tears,
with friendships formed and good times shared
and laughter through the years.

A life well-lived is a legacy of joy and pride and
pleasure, a loving, lasting memory
our grateful hearts will treasure.

THE DASH
Linda Ellis

I read of a man who stood to speak at the funeral of a friend. He
referred to the dates on his tombstone, from the beginning...
to the end. He noted that first came the date of his birth
and spoke of the following date with tears, but he said what
mattered most of all was the dash between those years

......More

SILENT TEAR

Author unknown

Just close your eyes and you will see
All the memories that you have of me
Just sit and relax and you will find
I'm really still there inside your mind
Don't cry for me now I'm gone
for I am in the land of song
there is no pain, there is no fear
so dry away that silent tear
Don't think of me in the dark and cold
For here I am, no longer old
I'm in that place that's filled with love
Known to you all, as "up above".

FOUR CANDLES

Author unknown

The first candle represents our grief.
The pain of losing you is intense.
It reminds us of the depth of our love for you.
This second candle represents our courage.
To confront our sorrow, to comfort each other,
To change our lives. This third candle we light in
your memory. For the times we laughed,
The times we cried, the times we were angry
with each other, the silly things you did,
The caring and joy you gave us.
This fourth candle we light for our love.
We light this candle that your light will always shine. As we enter
this holiday season and share this night of remembrance with our
family and friends. We cherish the special place in our hearts
that will always be reserved for you.
We thank you for the gift your living brought to
each of us. We love you. We remember you.

THE LIFE THAT I HAVE

Leo Marks

The life that I have
Is all that I have
And the life that I have is yours

The love that I have
Of the life that I have
Is yours and yours and yours

......More

SOFTLY
Author unknown

Softly, we felt you drift away,
But so FULL our hearts remain.
Although we longed for you to stay,
We must accept the pain.
We won't forget how brave you were,
As time kept moving on,
And just how much you fought and fought,
At last the pain has gone.
As we remain surrounded by your love,
We'll never forget what we had,
Your light will guide us from above,
Our protector, our guardian, our dad.
For you were much more than just a man,
A person we all shall miss,
And we'll tell you in the best way we can,
So much, but most of all this...
You were the pillar on which we proudly stood,
The person who created us all,
You always did as much as you could,
You caught us before we could fall.
You gave us our wings to fly on our own,
And taught us right from wrong,
But most of all, you've seen how we've grown,
And for you, we will always be strong.
So rest, please rest until we see you again,
In the gentle and welcoming calm,
For we will all be together then,
In your loving and welcoming arms.
Forever ours, Forever loved,
Forever missed.

TIME TO SAY GOODBYE, FOR
ALL FAMILY MEMBERS

Author unknown

When I'm alone I dream of the horizon and words fail me.
There is no light in a room where there is no sun and there
is no sun if you're not here with me, with me. From every
window unfurls my heart the heart that you have won.
Into me you've poured the light,
the light that you found by the side of the road.

Time to say goodbye. Places that I've never seen or experienced
with you. Now I shall, I'll sail with you upon ships across the
seas, seas that exist no more, it's time to say goodbye.

When you're far away I dream of the horizon and
words fail me. And of course I know that you're with
me, with me. You, my moon, you are with me. My sun,
you're here with me with me, with me, with me.

Time to say goodbye. Places that I've never seen or
experienced with you. Now I shall, I'll sail with you upon
ships across the seas, seas that exist no more,

I'll revive them with you. I'll go with you upon ships across the seas,
seas that exist no more, I'll revive them with you. I'll go with you.

REMEMBER ME

Margaret Mead

Remember me to the living, I am gone.
To the sorrowful, I will never return.
To the angry, I was cheated,
But to the happy, I am at peace,
And to the faithful, I have never left

......More

TO THOSE WHOM I LOVE

Alice Ramish

When I am gone, release me, let me go
I have so many things to see and do
You must not tie yourself to me with tears
Be happy that I have had so many years
I gave you my love, you can only guess
How much you gave me in happiness

......More

YOU'VE JUST WALKED ON AHEAD OF ME

Joyce Grenfell

And I've got to understand
You must release the ones you love
And let go of their hand

......More

THE ROSE BEYOND THE WALL

A.L. Frink

A rose once grew where all could see, sheltered beside a garden wall, and as the days passed swiftly by, it spread its branches, straight and tall. One day, a beam of light shone through a crevice that had opened wide, the rose bent gently toward its warmth then passed beyond to the other side. Now, you who deeply feel its loss, be comforted – the rose blooms there its beauty even greater now, nurtured by God's own loving care.

TURN AGAIN TO LIFE

Mary Lee Hall

If I should die, and leave you here awhile, be not like others sore
undone, who keep long vigils by the silent dust and weep.
For my sake, turn again to life, and smile,
Nerving thy heart and trembling hand to do
Something to comfort weaker hearts than thine.
Complete these dear unfinished tasks of mine,
And I, perchance, may therein comfort you!

WHEN I'M GONE

Lyman Hancock

When I come to the end of my journey
And I travel my last weary mile
Just forget if you can, that I ever frowned
And remember only the smile

Forget unkind words I may have spoken
Remember some good I have done
Forget that I ever had heartache
And remember I've had loads of fun

Forget that I've stumbled and blundered
And sometimes fell by the way
Remember I have fought some hard battles
And won, ere the close of the day

Then forget to grieve for my going
I would not have you sad for a day
But in summer just gather some flowers
And remember the place where I lay

And come in the shade of evening
When the sun paints the sky in the west
Stand for a few moments beside me
And remember only my best

WHEN WE ARE WEARY
Author unknown

When we are weary and in need of strength,
When we are lost and sick at heart,
We remember him. When we have a joy we crave to share,
when we have decisions that are difficult to make, when we
have achievements that are based on his, we remember him.
At the blowing of the wind and in the chill of winter
at the opening of the buds and in the rebirth of spring,
We remember him.
At the blueness of the skies and in the warmth of summer
at the rustling of the leaves and in the beauty of
autumn, we remember him. At the rising of the
sun and at its setting, we remember him.
As long as we live, he too will live for he is now
a part of us, as we remember him.

WHEN I AM GONE

Author unknown

When I am gone, mourn me not, peaceful sleep will be my lot

My life on earth its pleasure and its pain, has
been fairly balanced I cannot complain

Though perhaps my ideals it doesn't contain, my
friends are many, what more could I gain?

There is blessing in a world where there is love and care, There is
always hope and happiness, like the living life of a burning candle.

Or quietly singing a melodious song to a lonely broken heart, like
beautiful flowers to a garden, or rainy days after a long draught...
That it is you and me who care and can make a difference!

Although perhaps it's difficult today to see beyond the sorrow,
may looking back in memory help comfort you tomorrow.

If the future seems overwhelming, remember
that it comes one moment at a time.

INDIAN PRAYER

Author unknown

When I am dead
Cry for me a little
Think of me sometimes
But not too much.
Think of me now and again
As I was in life at some moments
It's pleasant to recall
But not for long.
Leave me in peace
And I shall leave you in peace
And while you live
Let your thoughts be with the living.

Other possible poems and readings

- Life is but a stopping place
- Look for me in rainbows
- Miss me but let me go – Tamara Moir
- Footprints
- If tears could build a stairway
- What makes a dad

SCRIPTURE VERSES

ECCLESIASTES 3:2-4

To everything there is a season, and a time
to every purpose under the heaven:

A time to be born, and a time to die; a time to plant, and a
time to pluck up that which is planted; a time to kill, and a
time to heal; a time to break down, and a time to build up;

A time to weep, and a time to laugh; a time
to mourn, and a time to dance.

1 CORINTHIANS 13

Love, it does not boast, it is not proud. It is not rude, it is not self-seeking, it is not easily angered, it keeps no record of wrongs.

Love does not delight in evil but rejoices with the truth. It always protects, always trusts, always hopes, and always perseveres.

JOHN 11:25–26

"I am the resurrection and the life," says the Lord. "Those who believe in me, even though they die, will live, and everyone who lives and believes in me will never die."

PSALM 23

The Lord is my shepherd, I shall not want. He makes me to lie down in green pastures: he leads me beside the still waters. He restores my soul: he leads me in the paths of righteousness for his name's sake. Yea, though I walk through the valley of the shadow of death, I will fear no evil: for thou art with me; thy rod and thy staff they comfort me. Thou prepares a table before me in the presence of mine enemies; thou anointest my head with oil; my cup runneth over. Surely goodness and mercy shall follow me all the days of my life. And I will dwell in the house of the Lord forever.

JOHN 14:1–6, 27

"Do not let your hearts be troubled. Trust in God; trust also in me.

In my Father's house are many rooms; if it
were not so, I would have told you.

I am going there to prepare a place for you.

And if I go and prepare a place for you, I will come back
and take you to be with me that you also may be where I
am. You know the way to the place where I am going."

Thomas said to him, "Lord, we don't know where
you are going, so how can we know the way?"

Jesus answered, "I am the way and the truth and the life.
No one comes to the Father except through me."

MATTHEW 5:4

Blessed are those who mourn, for they will be comforted.

LUKE 23:43

Jesus said, "Truly I tell you, today you will be with me in Paradise."

THESSALONIANS 4:14, 17B, 18

Since we believe that Jesus died and rose again, even
so, through Jesus, God will bring with him those
who have died. So we will be with the Lord for ever.
Therefore encourage one another with these words.

RELIGIOUS READINGS

> **66** *The only limit to our realisation of tomorrow will be our doubts of today. Let us move forward with strong and active faith.* **99**
> *– Franklin D. Roosevelt, President of the USA*

A BEAUTIFUL ANGEL

Christopher Warner

A beautiful angel is all that is here
Saying O Lord please leave me here
Not ready to leave but has to go
Wants to go back but God says no
A husband and children
Grandchildren and friends
A meaningful life that suddenly ends

......More

A THOUSAND WORDS

Author unknown

A thousand words won't bring you back, we know because we've tried. Neither will a thousand tears because they have been cried. Your memory is our keepsake, with which we'll never part, God has you in His keeping, and we have you in our hearts.

AN ANGEL NEVER DIES

Author unknown

Don't let them say I was never born, that something
stopped my heart, I felt each tender squeeze
you gave, I loved you from the start,

Although my body you can't hold, it doesn't mean I'm gone,
this world was worthy not of me, God chose that I move on,
I know the pain that drowns your soul, what you are forced
to face, you have my word, I'll fill your arms, and someday
we will embrace. You'll hear that it was "meant to be,
God doesn't make mistakes", but that won't soften your worst
blow, or make your heart not ache. I'm watching over all you do,
another child you'll bear, believe me when I say to you, that I am
always there. There will come a time I promise you, when you
will hold my hand, stroke my face, and kiss my lips, and you'll
understand. Although I no longer breathe your air, or gaze into
your eyes, that doesn't mean I never "was". An Angel never dies!

BROKEN CHAIN

Author unknown

We little knew that day God was going to call your name,
in life we loved you dearly, in death we do the same.

COME WITH ME

Rhonda Braswell

The Lord saw you getting tired and a cure was not to be, so
He put His arms around you and whispered, "Come to Me."

With tearful eyes, we watched you suffer
and saw you fade away, although we loved you
dearly, we could not make you stay.

A golden heart stopped beating, a beautiful smile
at rest, God broke our hearts to prove
He only takes the best.

It's lonesome here without you, we miss you so each
day, our lives aren't the same since you went away.

When days are sad and lonely, and everything goes wrong,
we seem to hear you whisper, "Cheer up and carry on."

Each time we see your picture, you seem to smile
and say, "Don't cry, I'm in God's keeping,
We'll meet again someday."

DO NOT STAND AT MY GRAVE AND WEEP

Mary Frye

Do not stand at my grave and weep
I am not there, I do not sleep.
I am a thousand winds that blow.
I am the diamond glints on snow.
I am the sunlight on ripened grain.
I am the gentle autumn rain.
When you awaken in the morning's hush
I am the swift uplifting rush
Of quiet birds in circled flight.
I am the soft stars that shine at night.
Do not stand at my grave and cry;
I am not there. I did not die.

DON'T GRIEVE FOR ME
Author unknown

Don't grieve for me, for now I'm free, I'm following the path
God laid for me. I took his hand when I heard his call, I
turned my back and left it all. I could not stay another day, to
laugh, to love, to work, to play. Tasks left undone must stay
that way, I've found that peace at the close of the day. If my
parting has left a void, then fill it with remembered joy.

A friendship shared, a laugh, a kiss, ah yes, these things I too
will miss. So be not burdened with times of sorrow, I wish you
the sunshine of tomorrow. My life's been full, I savoured much,

Good friends, good times, a loved one's touch, Perhaps my time
seemed all too brief, Don't lengthen it now with undue grief.

Lift up your heart and share with me,

God wanted me now, He set me free.

*Note: This poem is attributed to various authors and is also known by
several different titles*

DON'T CRY FOR ME (SPIRITS STORY)
Roisin Loughran

I know you are missing me, And I know you
are down, I know your heart's broken,
Because I'm not around, But I'm with you always, I'm deep in your
heart, I'm there with every breath you take, I didn't really depart,
I am sitting beside you

......More

GOD LOOKED UPON HIS GARDEN
Author Unknown

God looked around his garden
And found an empty place,
He then looked down upon the earth
and saw your tired face.
He put his arms around you
and lifted you to rest.
God's garden must be beautiful
He always takes the best.
He knew that you were suffering
He knew you were in pain.
He knew that you would never get well on earth again.
He saw the road was getting rough
and the hills were hard to climb.
So he closed your weary eyelids and whispered, "Peace be Thine".
It broke our hearts to lose you but you didn't go alone,
For part of us went with you
The day God called you home.

LIFE IS BUT A STOPPING PLACE
Maryam Kazmi

Life is but a stopping place,
a pause in what's to be, a resting place
along the road, to sweet eternity.

We all have different journeys,
Different paths along the way, we all were
meant to learn some things,
but never meant to stay

......More

THE DAY GOD TOOK YOU HOME
Author unknown

A million times I've needed you
A million times I've cried,
If love alone could have saved
You never would have died.
In life I loved you dearly;
In death I love you still.
In my heart you hold a space,
Where no one can ever fill.
It broke my heart to lose you,
But you didn't go alone
Part of me went with you,
the day God took you home.

THY KINGDOM COME
Lewis Hensley

Thy kingdom come, O God, Thy reign, O Christ, begin
Break with Thine iron rod the tyrannies of sin. Where
is Thy rule of peace and purity, and love?
When shall all hatred cease, as in the realms above?
When the promised time that war comes shall be no more,
Oppression, lust, and crime shall flee Thy face before?
We pray Thee, Lord, arise, and come in Thy great might;
Revive our longing eyes, which languish for Thy sight. Men
scorn Thy sacred name, And wolves devour Thy fold;
By many deeds of shame We learn that love grows
cold. O'er heathen lands afar Thick darkness broodeth
yet: Arise, O morning Star, Arise, and never set.

IF TEARS COULD BUILD A STAIRWAY
Paul Davis

If tears could build a stairway, and memories a
lane. I would walk right up to Heaven
and bring you back again. No farewell words
were spoken, No time to say "Goodbye"

......More

READINGS FOR FAMILY MEMBERS

For a child

TOO SOON
Mary Yarnall

No time to enjoy the world and its wealth
No time to take life down off the shelf
No time to sign the story of yourself
Though you had enough love for a lifetime

......More

CHILD
Author unknown

A sweet little flower, nipped in the bud,
No grief or sorrow knew;
Just came to earth to win our love
And then to heaven withdrew.
No stain was on her little heart,
Sin had not entered there;
And innocence slept sweetly on
That pale white brow so fair.
She was too pure for this cold earth
Too beautiful to stay,
And so God's holy angel bore
Our darling one away.

LOVE IS FOREVER
Author unknown

No words can ever take away
The pain and grief we feel each day,
No words can ever compromise
The flow of tears from saddened eyes.

No words can mend our broken hearts,
when tragically, we were torn apart.
But words are only words spoken... and quickly
gone, whilst memories are forever,
Living on and on and on.

We will never forget your little ways, or the twinkle in his eyes,
how you giggled, when you were tickled, and your smiles.

FOR ALL PARENTS

Edgar Guest (can be adapted for a girl as well)

"I'll lend you for a little time a child of mine," He said. "For
you to love the while he lives and mourn when he is dead,
It may be six or seven years, or twenty-two or three. But
will you, till I call him back, take care of him for me?
He'll bring his charms to gladden you, but should his stay be brief,
You'll have his lovely memories, as solace for your grief,
I cannot promise he will stay, since all from earth return,
But there are lessons taught down there I want this child to learn.
I've looked the wide world over in my search for teachers true,
And from the throngs that crowd life's lanes I have selected you.
Now will you give him all your love, nor think the labour vain,
Nor hate me when I come to call to take him back again?"
I fancied that I heard them say: "Dear Lord, Thy will be done!
For all the joy Thy child shall bring, the risk of grief we'll run.
We'll shelter him with tenderness: we'll love him while we may,
And for happiness we've known forever grateful stay. But should
the angels call for him much sooner than we'd planned.
We'll brave the bitter grief that comes and try to understand."

UPON A CHILD THAT DIED

Robert Herrick

Here she lies, a pretty bud,
Lately made of flesh and blood:
Who as soon as fell fast asleep
As her little eyes did peep.
Give her strewings, but not stir
The earth that lightly covers her.

SO GO AND RUN FREE

Author unknown

So go and run free with the angels
Dance around the golden clouds
For the Lord has chosen you to be with him
And we should feel nothing but proud
Although he has taken you from us
And our pain a lifetime will last
Your memory will never escape us
But make us glad for the time we did have
Your face will always be hidden
Deep inside our hearts
Each precious moment you gave us
Shall never, ever depart
So go and run free with the angels
As they sing so tenderly
And please be sure to tell them
To take good care of you for me

For a baby

HANDPRINT

Tony Doiron

You were lying in my arms, As I tried to say
goodbye, "It might be for the best," they said,
But I knew that was a lie. I gazed at your little
handprint, Given to us that day

......More

For a dad

(These can be adapted for grandfathers too.)

DADDY'S LITTLE GIRL
Pumpkin

If I had my life to do over,
I'd have chosen you to be my dad
once more. Even if it meant losing you again,
it's worth all the tears in the
world. You were my sunshine when skies
were gray. I loved you and honored you;
You took all my tears away.
I was happy to be with you,
Proud to be your little girl.
Sometimes we would argue,
But to me you meant the world.
Your love was always pure;
You treated me as your own.
Your time seemed all too short and
I feel so alone. What can I take from this?
My heart is completely crushed.
But nothing loved is ever lost –
And you are loved so much.

THE MAN IN THE ARENA

Theodore Roosevelt

It is not the critic who counts; not the man who points out how the strong man stumbles, or where the doer of deeds could have done them better. The credit belongs to the man who is actually in the arena, whose face is marred by dust and sweat and blood; who strives valiantly; who errs, who comes short again and again, because there is no effort without error and shortcoming; but who does actually strive to do the deeds; who knows great enthusiasms, the great devotions; who spends himself in a worthy cause; who at the best knows in the end the triumph of high achievement, and who at the worst, if he fails, at least fails while daring greatly, so that his place shall never be with those cold and timid souls who neither know victory nor defeat.

HE HAS ACHIEVED SUCCESS

Bessie A. Stanley

He has achieved success who has lived well, laughed often
and loved much: who has enjoyed the trust of pure women,
the respect of intelligent men and the love of little children;
who has filled the niche and accomplished his task; who has
left the world better than he found it; whether by an improved
poppy, a perfect poem, or a rescued soul; who has never lacked
appreciation of Earth's beauty or failed to express it; who has
always looked for the best in others and given the best he had.
Whose life was an inspiration; Whose memory now a benediction.

WHAT MAKES A DAD

Brie Carter

God took the strength of a mountain,
The majesty of a tree, The warmth of a summer
sun, The calm of a quiet sea, The generous soul
of nature, The comforting arm of night,
The wisdom of the ages.......
And so, He called it ... "DAD!"

......More

DAD

Author unknown

Dad we'll always remember
that special smile, that caring heart,
that warm embrace, you always gave us.
You being there for Mum and us
through good and bad times,
no matter what. We'll always remember
you Dad because they'll never be another
one to replace you in our hearts,
and the love we will always have for you.

HE IS GONE

David Harkins

You can shed tears that he has gone, or you can smile because
he has lived. You can close your eyes and pray that he will come
back, or you can open your eyes and see all that he has left

......More

DAD

Vicky Frye

If I could write a story it would be the greatest ever told
of a kind and loving father who had a heart of gold

......More

OUR FATHER KEPT A GARDEN
Author unknown

Our Father kept a garden.
A garden of the heart;
He planted all the good things,
That gave our lives their start.
He turned us to the sunshine,
and encouraged us to dream:
Fostering and nurturing the seeds of self-esteem.
And when the winds and rain came,
He protected us enough;
but not too much because he knew
we would stand up strong and tough.
His constant good example,
always taught us right from wrong;
Markers for our pathway that will last a lifetime long.
We are our Father's garden, we are his legacy.
Thank you Dad we love you.

THIS MODEST HERO
Author unknown

This modest hero held within
The gift to make a dumb heart sing
And fill that heart with the spirit of spring
This modest hero tore apart
The fences that separate heart from heart
And understood you from the start
This modest hero could read your soul
And mend the rift and make it whole
And set you to seek a better role.
His was a gift more precious than gold
Love that you give and still have and hold
To comfort the lost ones out in the cold.

For a soldier

THE SOLDIER

Rupert Brooke (1887–1915)

If I should die, think only this of me:
That there's some corner of a foreign field
That is forever England. There shall be
In that rich earth a richer dust concealed;
A dust that England bore, shaped, made aware,
Gave, once, her flowers to love, her ways to roam,
A body of England's, breathing English air,
Washed by the rivers, blest by suns of home.

And think, this heart, all evil shed away,
A pulse in the eternal mind, no less
Gives somewhere back the thoughts by England given;
Her sights and sounds; dreams happy as her day;
And laughter, learnt of friends; and gentleness,
In hearts at peace, under an English heaven.

For mums

66 *A mother holds her children's hands for a moment, but their hearts forever.* **99**
— Author unknown

LEGACY OF LOVE

Ruth C. Jurs

A wife, a mother, a grandma too,
This is the legacy we have from you.
You taught us love and how to fight,
You gave us strength, you gave us might.
A stronger person would be hard to find,
And in your heart, you were always kind.
You fought for us all in one way or another,
Not just as a wife not just as a mother.
For all of us you gave your best,

Now the time has come for you to rest.
So go in peace, you've earned your sleep,
Your love in our hearts, we'll eternally keep.

MISSING MY MUM

Chanda Robinson

I awake each morning to start a brand new day
But the pain of losing you never goes away
I go about the things I have to do
and as the hours pass I can't stop missing you,
I want to call you and just hear your voice
then I remember I have no choice; to accept the fact
that you are not here, and now my heart cries
just to see you again and tell you goodbye

.....More

ONE MOTHER

Jing Jing Lee

You can only have one mother,
Patient, kind and true;
No other friend in all the world,
Will be the same to you.
When other friends forsake you,
To mother you will return

......More

MOTHER
Author unknown

A wonderful mother, woman and aid,
one who was better God never made;
a wonderful worker, so loyal and true,
one in a million, that mother was you.
Just in your judgment, always right;
Honest and liberal, ever upright;
Loved by your friends and all whom you knew
our wonderful mother, that mother was you.

SHE HAS ACHIEVED SUCCESS
Bessie A. Stanley

You can shed tears that she has gone, or you can smile because she has lived. You can close your eyes and pray that she will come back, or you can open your eyes and see all that she has left.

Your heart can be empty because you can't see her, or you can be full of love that you shared. You can turn your back on tomorrow and live yesterday, or you can be happy for tomorrow because of yesterday.

You can remember her only that she is gone, or you can cherish her memory and let it live on. You can cry and close your mind, be empty and turn your back, or you can do what she would want: smile, open your eyes, love and go on.

OUR MUM
Michael Ashby

Where did it go?
My mother once asked
As the clock tick-tocked,
and her life flew past
In the race against time
She led for most of the way
But the track was endless
Unlike her last day
(Take care of your father
Promise you will
As she passed on the baton
She would never spill)
So polish the stars
And fire up the sun
And put out some slippers
To welcome my mum
Find a new galaxy
And light up her name
because life on planet Earth
Just won't be the same.

A MOTHER
Author unknown

A mother laughs our laughter. Sheds our tears, returns
our love, and fears our fears. She lives our joys. Cares
our cares. And all our hopes and dreams she shares.

OUR MOTHER KEPT A GARDEN OF THE HEART

Author unknown

Our Mother kept a garden.
A garden of the heart;
She planted all the good things,
that gave our lives their start.
She turned us to the sunshine,
and encouraged us to dream:
Fostering and nurturing the seeds of self-esteem.
And when the winds and rains came,
she protected us enough;
but not too much, because she knew
we'd need to stand up strong and tough.
Her constant good example,
always taught us right from wrong;

Markers for our pathway to last our whole life long.
We are our Mother's garden, we are her legacy.
And we hope today she feels the love, Reflected back from us.

MUMMY
Author unknown

We sat beside your bedside,
Our hearts were crushed and sore;
We did our best to the end,
'til we could do no more.
In tears we watched you sinking,
We watched you fade away;
And though our hearts were breaking,
We knew you could not stay.
You left behind some aching hearts,
That loved you most sincere;
We never shall and never will
Forget you Mother [Father] dear.

MY ROCK MY MUM
Del Abe Jones

Sometimes I catch myself thinking, "When I phone, I
can talk of this or that!" Then remember, I'm alone.
She was always there to answer my calls to listen to
my "small talk" or when I climbed the walls

......More

YOUR MOTHER IS ALWAYS WITH YOU

Author unknown

Your Mother is always with you.
She's the whisper of the leaves as you walk down the
street. She's the smell of certain foods you remember,
flowers you pick and perfume that she wore.
She's the cool hand on your brow when you're not feeling
well. She's your breath in the air on a cold winter's day.
She is the sound of the rain that lulls you to sleep, the colours of a
rainbow. She is Christmas morning.
Your Mother lives inside your laughter.
She's crystallized in every teardrop.
A mother shows every emotion ... happiness, sadness, fear,
jealousy, love, hate, anger, helplessness, excitement, joy,
sorrow... and all the while, hoping and
praying you will only know the good
feelings in life. She's the place you came
from, your first home, and she's
the map you follow with every step you take.
She's your first love; your first friend, even your
first enemy, but nothing on earth can separate
you. Not time, not space...not even death!

I WROTE YOUR NAME

Author unknown

I wrote your name in the sand, but the waves
washed it away. I wrote your name in the sky,
but the wind blew it away. So I wrote your name in
my heart, and that's where it will always stay.

HOW DO WE LET A MOTHER GO

Lori Boast

How do we let a mother go? How do we say "I'm ready now to go on without you"? How can we ever have a clue of what that really means? And of a sudden the moment is upon us, and there's no turning back

......More

For a grandmother

GRANDMOTHER
Author unknown

We had a wonderful Grandmother
One who never really grew old;
Her smile was made of sunshine,
And her heart was solid gold;
Her eyes were as bright as shining stars,
And in her cheeks fair roses you see.
We had a wonderful grandmother,
And that's the way it will always be.
But take heed, because
She's still keeping an eye on all of us,
So let's make sure
She will like what she sees.

NAN

Author unknown

Nan, your life was full of loving deeds,
Forever thoughtful of our special needs,
Today and tomorrow, our whole lives through,
we will always love and cherish you.
Those we love don't go away, they walk beside us every day, unseen,
unheard, but always near. Still loved, still missed and very dear.

GRANDMA

Augustine Perez

Thank you for the gift of love.
Now you're sharing it up above.
You had many things to say

......**More**

For a husband and a wife

MY HUSBAND
Author unknown

Always so good, unselfish and kind
none on this earth your equal I'll find.
Honourable and true in all your ways,
Loving and faithful to the end of your days,
Honest and liberal, ever upright,
Just in your judgment, always right;
Loved by your friends and all whom you knew,
One in a million, that husband was you.
As time has passed, our hearts still sore,
as time rolls on we miss you more;
a loving father, tender and kind.
What beautiful memories you left behind.

PARTINGS COME AND HEARTS ARE BROKEN
Author unknown

Partings come and hearts are broken,
Loved ones go with words unspoken,
Deep in our hearts there's a memory kept,
For a husband/wife and father/mother we'll never forget.
I've lost my life's companion,
A life linked with my own,
You're still mine to remember,
A husband/wife proud to call my own.

MY WIFE
Author unknown

These words dear wife are just for you, and come with love to say, I'm thinking of you constantly and miss you more each day. To lose you left me devastated but when I feel the pain I only have to close my eyes, and you are with me once again. For you made my life worth living, and although we are apart until I hold you once again you're safe within my heart.

For a son or daughter

SON OR DAUGHTER FROM MUM

Author unknown

There is a mother who misses you sadly,
And finds the time long since you went;
And I think of you daily and hourly,
But try to be brave and content.
But the tears that I shed in silence,
And breathe a sigh of regret,
For you were mine, and I remember,
Though all the world forget.

YOU ARE NEAR

Author unknown

You are near, even if I don't see you, you are with me, even if you are
far away. You are in my heart, in my thoughts, in my life, always.

MY SON

Lian Gell

Twilight draws ever closer through the window pane; I
look to heaven in hopes to see your smiling face again.
Memories, sweet memories are what keep you near; these
I treasure with all my heart – I hold them all so dear.
Remembering the love we shared and how it was taken
away; We never got to say goodbye on that fateful day.
One day we'll be together again – as I gaze up to the sky, I
thought that I could see you there, learning how to fly.

For an uncle

WHAT MAKES AN UNCLE?
Author unknown

An uncle is a special gift received from God above.
He starts out with kindness, then adds an abundance of love.
He taught you to so many things, just as if he were your dad.
You could talk to him about so many things,
just as if he were your dad.
You could talk to him about anything, then
suddenly things didn't seem so bad.
His devotion is unconditional, to that there is no end,
and as you get older, he becomes more like a friend.
He is always willing to help you, in any way that he can.
Watching you grow up, he was your biggest fan.
He has tremendous faith in you, he just has that special touch.
It's no wonder then dear uncle, why you are loved so much.

For an aunt

WE HAD A WONDERFUL AUNT
Author unknown

We had a wonderful Aunt, one who never really grew old:
Her smile was made of sunshine, and her heart was solid Gold:
Her eyes were as bright as shining stars, and
in her cheeks fair roses you see.
We had a wonderful Aunt, and that's the way it will always
be. But take heed, because she's still keeping an eye on all
of us, so let's make sure she will like what she sees.

MY AUNTIE
George Naylor

When I was hopeless, you were there.
You picked me up, you showed me care.
Without the love you had for me
God only knows where I would be

......**More**

For a brother

FOR A BROTHER
Author unknown

In memory of a special brother, so full of loving deeds,
who always thought of others first, and helped fulfill their needs,
someone who loved to bring a smile as he went on his way,
and never failed to brighten up a dark and gloomy day,
someone who'll never know how much
he's missed and thought about
for when he left, it seemed as if the stars had all gone out,
brother you meant so very much, in every single way,
and you're remembered with much love, today and every day.

IN MEMORY OF A SPECIAL BROTHER
Author unknown

Today is full of memories, of a brother laid to rest and
every single one of them is filled with happiness.
For you were someone special, always such a joy to know and
there was so much pain, when it was time to let you go.
That's why this special message, is sent to heaven above, for
the angels to take care of you and give you all my love.

For a sister

SISTER

Morgan Martinez

One day it happened
In a blink of an eye
So sadly her life ended
Without a chance to say goodbye
She was such a happy girl
With a beautiful smile
Without a care in the world
She made it worthwhile

......More

66 *A sister is a gift to the heart,
a friend to the spirit, a golden
thread to the meaning of life.* 99
— Isadora James

SLEEP, MY SISTER

T. Hutchinson

I wish you sweet sleep, my sister dear.
Although there's so much that you've left bare,
I hate that you had to endure such pain.
On my mind, your saddened eyes have left a stain.

......More

For a friend

FAREWELL MY FRIENDS

Rabindranath Tagore

Farewell My Friends
It was beautiful
As long as it lasted
The journey of my life.
I have no regrets whatsoever save
The pain I'll leave behind.
Those dear hearts who love and care...
And the strings pulling at the heart and soul...
The strong arms that held me up
When my own strength let me down.
At the turning of my life I came across
Good friends,
Friends who stood by me
Even when time raced me by.
Farewell, farewell my friends
I smile and
Bid you goodbye.
No, shed no tears
For I need them not
All I need is your smile.
If you feel sad
Do think of me
For that's what I'll like
When you live in the hearts
Of those you love
Remember then
You never die.

This section may be of help to families who have had the extra heartache of losing a loved one through the trauma of suicide.

A WISH AND A PRAYER

Lauren

May your spirit soar in freedom
from the fears that gripped so tight.
May you find the peace you searched for
as you wandered, lost, in the night.
May your tortured mind be clear and calm
and your tender heart be warm.
May you have no need for strength now

......More

WHAT IT TAKES

Biff Rushton

What it takes, they all think they know, they mention Selfishness,
Courage, Cowardice, Desperation, Insanity, Fatigue.
Others throw around Impulsiveness, Control and Weakness.
Everyone knows, but they don't understand
what it takes, what it really takes.
More than anything else, is Pain, A world of Pain

......More

WE THOUGHT THAT YOU WERE HAPPY

Author unknown

We thought that you were happy,
we must have all been blind,
we didn't know your suffering
we didn't know your mind,
You have left all our hearts aching
and we are not sure how we'll cope
if only you had talked it over
we may have found you hope.

We thought that you were happy
but yours was a troubled mind
hardly a hint, hardly a clue
how could we be so blind?

You chose to go from this place
and onto somewhere new
may you find peace at last
our love goes with you.

RELEASE OF DOVES READINGS

LITTLE DOVE

Author unknown

On the wings of this white dove I'll set your spirit free.
Up into the big deep sky, to heaven, where you'll be.
I know God has a plan for us, he wants us by his side.
But it is hard for us to understand when we are left behind.
Little dove, help lift our hearts as we watch you go,
God is there if we just ask, because He loves us so.

TWO DOVES

Author unknown

Two Doves meet in the Sky,
Two loves hand in hand, eye to eye,
Two parts of a living soul
Two stars shining big and bright,
Two fires bringing warmth and light
Two loves free without a care,
Two hearts but now a single soul.

BUTTERFLIES

Jill Haley

As you release this butterfly in honour of me,
know that I'm with you and will always be.
Hold a hand, say a prayer, close your eyes and see me there.
Although you may feel a bit torn apart,
please know that I'll be forever in your heart.
Now fly away butterfly as high as you can go, I'm
right there with you more than you know.

A BUTTERFLY LIGHTS BESIDE US

Author unknown

A butterfly lights beside us, like a sunbeam...
And for a brief moment its glory and beauty belong to our
world... but then it flies on again, and although we wish it
could have stayed, we are so thankful to have seen it at all.

66 *Do not pray for an easy life, pray for
the strength to endure a difficult one.* 99
– Bruce Lee

NAUTICAL RELATED READINGS

CROSSING THE BAR

Alfred, Lord Tennyson

Sunset and evening star,
And one clear call for me!
And may there be no moaning of the bar,
When I put out to sea,
But such a tide as moving seems asleep,
Too full for sound and foam,
When that which drew from out the
boundless deep turns again home.
Twilight and evening bell, And after that the dark!
And may there be no sadness or farewell, when I embark;
For tho' from out our bourne of Time and
Place the flood may bear me far,
I hope to see my Pilot face to face when I have crost the bar.

I AM STANDING ON THE SEASHORE

Bishop Brent

I am standing upon the seashore. A ship, at my side, spreads her
white sails to the moving breeze and starts for the blue ocean.
She is an object of beauty and strength.
I stand and watch her until, at length, she hangs like a speck
of white cloud just where the sea and sky
come to mingle with each other.

Then, someone at my side says, "There, she is gone."

Gone where? Gone from my sight. That is
all. She is just as large in mast,
hull and spar as she was when she left my side.
And, she is just as able to bear her load of
living freight to her destined port.

Her diminished size is in me – not in her.
And, just at the moment when someone says, "There, she is gone,"
there are other eyes watching her coming, and other voices
ready to take up the glad shout, "Here she comes!" And that
is dying. Death comes in its own time, in its own way.

SEA FEVER

John Masefield

I must go down to the seas again, to the lonely sea and the sky,
And all I ask is a tall ship and a star to steer her by

......More

NORTH SHIP

Philip Larkin

I saw three ships go sailing by,
Over the sea, the lifting sea,
And the wind rose in the morning sky,
And one was rigged for a long journey.

The first ship turned towards the west,
Over the sea, the running sea,
And by the wind was all possessed
And carried to a rich country.

The second turned towards the east,
Over the sea, the quaking sea,
And the wind hunted it like a beast
To anchor in captivity.

The third ship drove towards the north,
Over the sea, the darkening sea,
But no breath of wind came forth,
And the decks shone frostily.

The northern sky rose high and black
Over the proud unfruitful sea,
East and west the ships came back
Happily or unhappily:

But the third went wide and far
Into an unforgiving sea
Under a fire-spilling star,
And it was rigged for a long journey.

THE SEA SPIRIT

Madison Julius Cawein

Ah me! I shall not waken soon
From dreams of such divinity!
A spirit singing 'neath the moon
　　to me.

Wild sea-spray driven of the storm
is not as wildly white as she,
Who beckoned with a foam-white arm?
　　To me.

With eyes dark green, and golden-green
Long locks that rippled drippingly,
Out of the green wave she did lean
　　To me.

And sang; till Earth and Heaven seemed
A far, forgotten memory,
And more than Heaven in her who gleamed
　　On me.

Sleep, sweeter than love's face or home;
And death's immutability;
And music of the plangent foam,
　　For me!

Sweep over her! With all thy ships,
With all thy stormy tides, O sea!
The memory of immortal lips
　　For me!

NATURAL BURIAL READINGS

WOODLAND BURIAL

Pam Ayres

Don't lay me in some gloomy churchyard shaded by a wall
Where the dust of ancient bones has spread a dryness over all,
Lay me in some leafy loam where, sheltered from the
cold, Little seeds investigate and tender leaves unfold

......More

MY WOODED WORLD

Sheila Visingardi

As a child, I would sit and ponder, at the wooded areas, for their
beauty relaxed me. The sway of the branches and whistling of the
winds, as if they were calling my name. Then as I grew older, they
were my retreat, for the woods became my own world. A world full
of imagination, creativity, resourcefulness, as well as inspiration

......More

DO NOT STAND AT MY GRAVE AND WEEP

Mary Frye

Do not stand at my grave and weep
I am not there, I do not sleep.
I am a thousand winds that blow.
I am the diamond glints on snow.
I am the sunlight on ripened grain.
I am the gentle autumn rain.
When you awaken in the morning's hush
I am the swift uplifting rush
Of quiet birds in circled flight.
I am the soft stars that shine at night.
Do not stand at my grave and cry;
I am not there. I did not die.

THEMED READINGS

For fishermen

FOR A FISHERMAN
Author unknown

Just as the mist it rises
Then vanishes way down the stream
[insert name] too has come and then left us
Today it seems like a dream
That he was so much part of our lives
That he lived and loved as we do
Now he has left our hearts and his home
Like the fish that a fisherman threw
Back in the stream to go on its way
And that is what **[insert name]** is doing today
To a bright new world, see the sun glitter
As he drifts from sight, though our tears are bitter
We know that he, like the salmon's leap
Will always be there in our memories deep.

GONE FISHIN'

Delmar Pepper

So put me on a boat headed out to sea.
Please send along my fishing pole
For I've been invited to the fishin' hole.
Where every day is a day to fish,
To fill your heart with every wish.
Don't worry, or feel sad for me,
I'm fishin' with the Master of the sea.
We will miss each other for a while,
But you will come and bring your smile.
That won't be long you will see,
Till we're together you and me.
To all of those that think of me,
Be happy as I go out to sea.
If others wonder why I'm missin'
Just tell 'em I've gone fishin'.

For golfers

FOR A GOLFER
Allan Berman

In my hand I hold a ball,
White and Dimpled, Rather Small.
Oh, How Bland It Does Appear,
This Harmless Looking Little Sphere.

By Its Size I Could Not Guess,
The Awesome Strength It Does Possess.
But Since I Fell beneath Its Spell,
I've wandered through the Fires of Hell.

My Life Has Not Been Quite the Same,
Since I Chose To Play This Stupid Game.
It Rules My Mind for Hours On End,
A Fortune It Has Made Me Spend.

It Has Made Me Yell, Curse and Cry,
I Hate Myself And Want To Die.
It Promises a Thing Called Par,
If I Can Hit It Straight And Far.

To Master Such a Tiny Ball,
Should Not Be Very Hard At All.
But My Desires the Ball Refuses,
And Does Exactly As It Chooses.

It Hooks and Slices, Dribbles and Dies,
and Even Disappears Before My Eyes.
Often It Will Have A Whim,
To Hit A Tree Or Take A Swim.

With Miles of Grass on Which to Land,
It Finds A Tiny Patch Of Sand.
Then Has Me Offering Up My Soul,
If Only It Would Find The Hole.

It's Made Me Whimper like A Pup,
And Swear That I Will Give It Up.
And Take to Drink to Ease My Sorrow,

But The Ball Knows ...
I'll Be Back Tomorrow.
Or perhaps not!

For dancers

I AM A DANCER
Author unknown

I am a dancer. I twirl, leap, and spin. I jump,
pirouette, and tap. I am a dancer. I feel pain and
fear. I feel defeat and failure. Yet, I keep going.

I smile, I practise, and I perform. I have grace and
beauty. I do not dance because I am happy, I am happy
because I dance. I hear the applause. I perform and
do my best. Sometimes I fail. I don't give up.

For I am a dancer. I am brave and strong. I dance
not for fame and glory. But for how I feel inside. I am
happiness, joy, love, and excitement. Strife, talent,
joy. Determination and beauty. I am a dancer.

BLESSINGS

GAELIC BLESSING

Deep peace of the running wave to you.
Deep peace of the flowing air to you.
Deep peace of the quiet earth to you.
Deep peace of the shining stars to you.
Deep peace of the gentle night to you.
Moon and stars pour their healing light on you. Deep
peace of Christ, of Christ the light of the world to you.
Deep peace of Christ to you.

IRISH BLESSING

May the roads rise up to meet you,
May the wind be always at your back.
May the sun shine warm upon your face,
May the rains fall soft upon fields.
And until we meet again
May God hold you in the palm of his hand.

HERE'S TO BEEFSTEAK

Here's to beefsteak, when you are hungry, whiskey when you are dry, all the women you'll ever need and Heaven when you die.

*There are blessings,
everyday.
Find them.
Create them.
Treasure them.*

COMMENDATION AND FAREWELL

This can be adapted and personalised for the departed, and is for a non-religious service, and can be used by a humanist Celebrant.

There is blessing in a world where there is love and care,
There is always hope and happiness,
Like the living life of a burning candle,
Or quietly singing a melodious song to a lonely broken heart,
Like beautiful flowers to a garden,
Or rainy days after a long drought...
That it is you and me who care and can make a difference!

They say there is a reason,
they say that time will heal,
But neither time nor reason,
Will change the way we feel.

There is a time for everything,
and a season for every activity under the heavens:
A time to be born and a time to die.
A time to laugh, and a time to weep, a time
to dance, and a time to mourn.
Sadly today is a time to weep and mourn for **[Name]**.

So into the freedom of the wind and sunshine we let you go into
the dance of the stars and the planets, we let you go into the
wind's breath, and the hands of the starmaker we let you go.

[Name] you were always greatly loved and respected, you always
will be, you will be greatly missed, you had a gift to make
people laugh and feel good about themselves. The memories of
you will always live on. So rest in peace and go safely home.

> **" Those we love don't go away, they
> walk beside us every day. Unseen,
> unheard but always near, still loved
> still missed, and forever dear. "
> – Author unknown**

PRARYERS

WALK IN GOD'S SUNSHINE
Author unknown

May you always walk in sunshine and
God's love around you flow, for the
Happiness you gave us, no one will
Ever know, it broke our hearts to lose
You, but you did not go alone, a part
Of us went with you, the day God
Called you home.
A million times we've needed you.
A million times we've cried.
If love could only have saved you.
You never would have died.
The Lord be with you and
May You Rest in Peace. Amen.

THE LORD'S PRAYER

Our Father who art in heaven,
hallowed be your name,
your kingdom come,
your will be done,
on earth as it is in heaven.
Give us today our daily bread.
Forgive us our trespasses
as we forgive those who trespass against us.
Lead us not into temptation
but deliver us from evil.
For thine is the kingdom, the power,
and the glory are yours
now and for ever. Amen.

Prayers for those who have suffered with Alzheimer's

YOU DIDN'T DIE JUST RECENTLY
Dick Underwood

You didn't die just recently, you died some time ago.
Although your body stayed a while, and didn't really know.
For you had got Alzheimer's, you failed to comprehend.
Your body went on living. But your mind had reached its end.
So we've already said, "Goodbye", to the person that we knew.
The person that we truly loved, the person that was, "You".
And so we meet again today, to toast your body's end.
For it was true and faithful, until right at the end. And
now, when we remember, we'll think of all the rest.
We'll concentrate on earlier, and remember all the best. For
in the real scheme of things, your illness wasn't long.
Compared to all the happiness, you brought your whole life
long. We think of you as yesterday, when you were fit and well.
And when we're asked about you, it's those things that we'll tell.
And so we meet in remembrance, of a mind so fit and true.
We're here to pay our last respects, to say that, "We love you".

POUR YOUR GRACE

Author unknown

Pour your grace, O loving God, upon all suffering with dementia.
It is frustrating not to find a word; it is
fearful to lose one's memories.
Bless them with patience, a loving and supporting family, and
days of hope and accomplishment. In Christ's name we pray.
Amen.

WE SEEM TO GIVE THEM BACK TO THEE

William Penn

We seem to give them back to Thee, O God who Gavest them to us.
Yet as Thou didst not lose them in giving,
So do we not lose them by their return?
Not as the world giveth, givest Thou O Lover of souls.
What Thou givest Thou takest not away,
For what is Thine is ours also if we are thine.
And life is eternal and love is immortal,
And death is only a horizon,
And a horizon is nothing save the limit of our sight.
Lift us up, strong Son of God that we may see further;
Cleanse our eyes that we may see more clearly;
Draw us closer to Thyself
That we may know ourselves to be nearer to
our loved ones who are with Thee.
And while Thou dost prepare a place for us,
prepare us also for that happy place,
That where Thou art we may be also for evermore.

Other specific prayers

THE LANDLORD'S PRAYER
Author unknown

Our lager, which art in barrels, hallowed be thy drink.
Thy will be drunk (I will be drunk), at home as it is in the
tavern. Give us this day our foamy head, and forgive us our
spillage, as we forgive those who spill against us. And lead
us not to incarceration, but deliver us from hangovers.
For thine is the spirit, the bitter, and the
lager. Forever and ever, Barmen.

PRAYER TO ST. GENESIUS, PATRON OF ACTORS

Author unknown

Dear Genesius, according to a very ancient story when you were still a pagan you once ridiculed Christ while acting on the stage. But, like Saul on the road to Damascus, you were floored by Christ's powerful grace. You rose bearing witness to Jesus and died a great martyr's death. Intercede for your fellow actors before God, that they may faithfully and honestly perform their roles and so help others to understand their role in life thus enabling them to attain their end in heaven. Amen.

THE CUB SCOUT PRAYER
Author unknown

Help us, oh lord, to serve you day by day
to do our duty and to enjoy our play
to keep the Cub Scout promise and to rest
Knowing we tried to do our best. Amen.

PRAYER FOR FIRE FIGHTERS
Author unknown

Merciful Father in heaven, look down in your love upon all those who protect us and ours from the ravages of fire and flame. Grant them the courage and skills to carry out their duties well and safely. When they must go into the face of danger, be by their side in the smoke and flames. Watch over their families, ever reminding them that those who fight fire are also in your loving care. This we ask in the name of Jesus Christ, our Lord and Saviour. Amen.

PRAYER FOR POLICE OFFICERS
Author unknown

Almighty God, Whose great power and eternal
Wisdom embraces the universe,
Watch over all policemen and Law
enforcement officers everywhere.
Protect them from harm in the performance of their duty
To stop crime, robbery, riots and violence.
We pray, help them keep our streets and homes safe, day and night.
We commend them to your loving care
because their duty is dangerous.
Grant them strength and courage in their daily assignments.
Dear God, protect these brave men and women.
Grant them your almighty protection,
Unite them safely with their families after Duty has
ended. Please God, grant us this wish. Amen.

Prayers for military personnel

ROYAL NAVY PRAYER

Author unknown

Go forth into the world in peace: be of good courage;
hold fast that which is good; render no man evil for evil;
strengthen the fainthearted; support the weak; help
the afflicted; honour all men; love and serve the Lord,
rejoicing in the power of the Holy Spirit. Amen.

SUBMARINER'S PRAYER

Author unknown

Almighty, Everlasting God, and the Protector of all those who put
their trust in Thee: hear our prayers in behalf of Thy servants
who sail their vessels beneath the seas. We beseech Thee to keep
in Thy sustaining care all who are in submarines, that they may
be delivered from the hidden dangers of the deep. Grant them
courage, and a devotion to fulfil their duties, that they may better
serve Thee and their native land. Though acquainted with the
depths of the ocean, deliver them from the depths of despair and
the dark hours of the absence of friendliness and grant them a good
ship's spirit. Bless all their kindred and loved ones from whom they
are separated. When they surface their ships, may they praise Thee
for Thou art there as well as in the deep. Fill them with Thy Spirit
that they may be sure in their reckonings, unwavering in duty,
high in purpose, and upholding the honour of their nation. Amen.

PRAYER FOR AIRBORNE FORCES
Author unknown

May the defence of the Most High be above
and beneath, around and within us,
in our going out and in our coming in,
in our rising up and our going down,
all our days and all our nights,
until the dawn when the son of righteousness shall
arise with healing in his wings for the peoples of the
world through Jesus Christ our Lord. Amen.

THE PILOT'S PRAYER
Author unknown

Oh controller, who sits in tower
Hallowed be thy sector.
Thy traffic come, thy instructions be done
on the ground as they are in the air.
Give us this day our radar vectors,
and forgive us our poor R/T
As we forgive those who cut us off on final.
And lead us not into adverse weather,
but deliver us our clearances.
For thine is the Tower, the approach and the centre, for
until you disconnect, for ever and ever ..... Out.

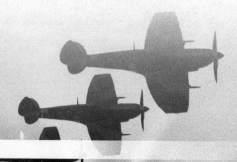

THE LAST POST

Author unknown

Day is done, gone the sun,
From the lakes, from the hills, from the sky
All is well, safely rest, God is nigh.

Fading light dims the sight.
And a star gems the sky, gleaming bright.
From afar, drawing nigh, falls the night.

Thanks and praise, for our days,
Neath the sun, neath the stars, neath the sky
As we go, this we know, God is nigh.

> **66** *Time is too slow for those who wait; Too swift for those who fear; Too long for those who grieve; Too short for those who rejoice; But for those that love; Time is eternity.* **99**
> *– Henry Van Dyke*

PRECIOUS MEMORY

Author unknown

The rain may wash my pain away
The wind may dry my tears
The summer sun may heal my heart
And time subdue my fears
But nothing in the world below
Or in the Heavens above
Will ever take away
The precious memory of your love.

Before the planned meeting with the Minister or Celebrant, the family can hopefully use the content of this book in the privacy of their own home, to discuss and perhaps seek opinion from relatives not able to attend the meeting, about the service most suited to celebrate the life of their departed love one.

CHARITABLE DONATIONS ON BEHALF OF A LOVED ONE

As I have mentioned, many families choose to ask friends and families to make donations to their chosen or preferred charities to honour their loved one, instead, or as well as, giving floral tributes on the day of the funeral. Their chosen charity is usually named on the back of an Order of Service or printed with the funeral notice in the local paper.

Funeral Directors will accept the donations, however charitable gifts may also be made direct to charities. Perhaps one or more of the following leading charities may be suitable?

Donations can usually be made by phone, post or online to the following:

Alzheimer's Society
43-44 Crutched Friars
London, EC3N 2AE
Telephone: 0330 333 0804
www.alzheimers.org.uk

British Heart Foundation
180 Hampstead Road,
Greater London House,
London NW1 7AW
Telephone: 0300 330 3322
www.bhf.org.uk

Cancer Research UK
PO Box 1561
Oxford OX4 9G
Telephone: 0300123 1022
www.cancerresearchuk.org

Help for Heroes
Unit 14 Parkers Close,
Downton Business Centre,
Salisbury, Wiltshire SP 53RB
Telephone: 0300 030 9888
www.helpforheroes.org.uk

Hospice UK
34–44 Britannia Street
London WC1X 9JG
Telephone: 020 7520 8200
www.hospiceuk.org

RNLI
West Quay Road, Poole
Dorset BH15 1HZ
Telephone: 0300 3009 990
www.rnli.org

Stroke Association
Supporter care team
1 Sterling Business Park,
Salt House Road,
Northampton, NN4 7EX.
Telephone: 0300 3300 740
www.stroke.org.uk

ABOUT THE AUTHOR

Paul Hickman trained as a Reader (Lay Minister) in the Church of England for three years before being licensed in Portsmouth Cathedral in 2000.

He served in the ministry team at St John the Baptist Church, Rowlands Castle in Hampshire for nine years. He left to serve bereaved families outside the institutional church, assisting them through the unique and personal heartbreak of losing a loved one, by helping to plan and conduct funeral services.

During his time in the Church, Paul conducted numerous burial and crematorium services, including his own father's.

Over the years, Paul has now served over 800 families, with religious and non-religious services, memorial services, and burial of ashes, in churches, crematoriums and natural burial sites, including the service of his best friend of over 57 years.

Over these years he has served families who have experienced the heartbreak of losing babies, mums, dads, granddads and grandmothers, brothers, sisters, war heroes, military veterans, centenarians and sadly suicides.

It is this experience serving families, meeting them for the first time in their homes over the years, having been appointed by the family's chosen Funeral Director, that has led him to publish this book, to try and ease the painful funeral planning process, and to reflect and celebrate their lives.

Although in many cases families do have an idea of what they want to include within the service, in most cases families need gentle guidance. To many people at this challenging time, the thought of trawling through the internet, or looking at orders of service compiled by other bereaved families, to find material that meets their needs, can be a very difficult experience.

This is where the Minister or Celebrant uses their own experience to guide the family.

That is why he is hoping this book will be of great assistance to Funeral Directors, nursing homes, and registry offices as they support their families, and of course the bereaved families, to help ease the burden of this important aspect of the grieving process.

TESTIMONIALS FOR THE AUTHOR

Although these testimonials are personal to the author, they represent the quality of feedback, and are typical of that given to Ministers and Celebrants throughout the country, who support families on a daily basis.

I just wanted to thank you on behalf of my family for the impeccable job that you made of our dad's service today. Many people commented on how you carried it out so well. It felt very personal and heartfelt and in no way clinical like many services can be. You did us proud and we are all so very grateful to you. **Kind regards, Vince and family.**

On behalf of my family and myself, I want to say a very big thank you to you, for the fantastic service that you delivered for Mum and us last Thursday. All of those in attendance said how good the service and your delivery was. Perfect. **Kind Regards, Barry.**

Julie and I would like to thank you for the service and the support you gave us at Mum's funeral last Monday. You conveyed everything in such a personal way and everyone has said what a lovely service it was. We cannot thank you enough for making the day run so smoothly. **Kind regards, Terri.**

My sincere thanks for the wonderful service you gave us all last Monday for Clem's final departure. My tears were not only for Clem but for you too, as they were tears of happiness felt by the sympathy that you showed and by the way you presented the service so absolutely perfect from beginning to end. Every single person commented on how everything had been so perfectly performed. "The best cremation service" for those who had already been to many this year alone. The doves obviously put the final perfect touch accompanied by your lovely words. It was a real pleasure to meet you and I am pleased to say that my whole family and friends were very pleased with you. I wish you happiness and success and again Paul, many thanks for everything. **All my very best wishes, Colette.**

I just wanted to drop a brief line to thank you very much for your kindness and solicitude on Friday afternoon. It must be a difficult and unenviable task to conduct funerals for persons unknown to you. You demonstrated a warmth and intimacy during the proceedings indicative of a close personal acquaintance with Dad – a rare skill. We were very fortunate that Bonnie was able to secure your services and entrust the proceedings to your pastoral care. I believe my father would have been very satisfied and would have marked you down in his diary as "a thoroughly decent chap"! Once again, a pleasure to have met you, and my sincere thanks again for your help on a very taxing day. **With kind regards, Sallie.**

Thank you so much for your support and care for our family during the loss of our dad and granddad David. We were comforted by your messages of hope and kindness.

It was a lovely service. **Denise, Eric, Ashley and Laura. x**

I would just like to say on behalf of my mum and myself what a good send-off you gave my dad yesterday. It was a very good service and Mum was very pleased with the content of the service, so once again I would like to say a very big thank you. **Andrew.**

On behalf of my mum and family we would like to say a big thank you on your professional and kind way you explained everything to us the other day. It put my mum at ease. Thank you very much.

I read out the words to the draft Order of Service to my mum and we both agreed it was so beautiful. **Kim.**

SCATTER MY ASHES TO THE WIND

Author unknown

To help the flowers grow. If you must bury something, let it be my faults, my weaknesses, and all my prejudice against my fellow man. Give my soul to God. If by chance you wish to remember me, do it with a kind deed or word to someone who needs you. If you do all I have asked, I will live forever.

SERVICE CONFIRMATION

Service date: _____

Service time: _____

Place of service: _____

Appointed minister or celebrant for the service:

_____

Selected music choices for entry, reflection and exit:

1) _____

2) _____

3) _____

Selected Hymn(s) if required:

1) _____

2) _____

Selected readings:

1) _____ Page _____

2) _____ Page _____

3) _____ Page _____

Selected prayer(s) if required:

1) _____ Page _____

2) _____ Page _____

NOTES

NOTES

Lightning Source UK Ltd.
Milton Keynes UK
UKHW021108110122
396955UK00005B/47

9 781916 241107